THE MASTER MIND

To the members and numerous friends of

DORNOCH CATHEDRAL

on the occasion of the Cathedral's

750th ANNIVERSARY

Let this mind be in you
which was also in Jesus Christ
PHILIPPIANS 2:5

THE
MASTER MIND

Jesus according to his enemies

JAMES A. SIMPSON

The Handsel Press
1988

Published by
The Handsel Press Ltd.
33 Montgomery Street, Edinburgh

ISBN 0 905312 86 4

First published 1988

© 1988 The Handsel Press Ltd.

New English Bible © 1970 by permission of
Oxford and Cambridge University Presses.

British Library Cataloguing in Publication Data
Simpson, James A. (James Alexander), 1934-
    The master mind.
    1. Jesus Christ
    I. Title
    232

    ISBN 0-905312-86-4

Printed by
W. M. Bett Ltd, Tillicoultry, Scotland

Contents

No other life lived on this planet has been so potent in the affairs of men. . . . From Jesus, through Christianity, have issued impulses which have helped to shape every phase of civilisation.

KENNETH SCOTT LATOURETTE, *The Unquenchable Light*

Of what I have learnt from the Gospels in the course of my long task [*of translating them*] I will say only this, that they bear the seal of the Son of Man and God, they are the Magna Carta of the human spirit. Were we to devote to their comprehension a little of the selfless enthusiasm that is now expended on the riddle of our physical surroundings, we should cease to say that Christianity is coming to an end—we might even feel it had only just begun.

E. V. RIEU, *The Four Gospels*

I find more awe in my soul when I come before Christ with all my faculties alert, than when I stand on a hilltop of a summer's night and gaze out into the fathomless space between the stars. . . .

A grim sort of failure he was on the cross; but from that day to this it has been better to fail with him than to succeed with the people whose business it is in every generation to nail him there.

PAUL SCHERER, *Love is a Spendthrift*

It is only the petty in us which is against Jesus Christ. All that is great in us is on his side.

ADOLPHE MONOD

Preface

In his account of the trial of Jesus, Mark tells how, after the Roman soldiers had finished mocking Jesus, 'they stripped him of the royal purple and dressed him in his own clothes'. This modest volume is an attempt to do something similar—to remove some of the ecclesiastical millinery and theological embroidery in which the Galilean carpenter has been dressed during the past two thousand years.

I hope this book may help those, for whom Jesus has become an enigma, to see him 'in his own clothes', more as his contemporaries saw him, and to glimpse from that picture something of the original grandeur and dynamism of Jesus of Nazareth, and his uniqueness.

Life-enrichment being central to the ministry and message of Jesus, I have not hesitated to remind the reader of the crucial importance of Jesus' life and teaching for our modern world. I believe any worthwhile book about Jesus must also be about life.

I gratefully acknowledge my indebtedness to Mary Millican and the Very Rev. Dr Andrew Doig for their encouragement and their careful reading of the manuscript. Any faults or heresies that remain are mine, not theirs. In quoting from the Bible, I have mainly used the New English Bible translation.

JAMES A. SIMPSON

Introduction

In the village church at Ystad, on the shores of the Baltic, there is a life-size crucifix, directly facing the pulpit. The head of Christ has human matted hair, the crown is of real thorns. How it came there is of remarkable interest. In 1716 Charles XII, King of Sweden, then at the peak of his fame, nationally and internationally, attended morning worship in the little church. He came unheralded. The minister, taken unawares, thought fit to put aside his prepared sermon and instead paid a glowing tribute to the king. Several weeks later, there was delivered to the church the great crucifix, and this message of Royal Command:

> *This is to hang on the pillar opposite the pulpit so that all who stand there shall be reminded of their proper subject.*

How relevant this reminder is two centuries later. Still in the pulpit we have too many words that never touch that 'proper subject'. When Dietrich Bonhoeffer, the German martyr, set down his explanation of the weakness of the Church in Nazi Germany, he wrote, 'Ecclesiastical interests well to the fore, but little interest in Christ'.

In an age like ours when unbelief has suddenly found its voice and speaks with bold assurance, it is essential that Christians should be able to speak with reasonable clarity and understanding about Jesus, his person, character, convictions, principles and Spirit. He is central to Christianity and to the working out of God's purposes in history.

The Gospels are our main source for learning about him. There we have the record of the different impressions Jesus made on his contemporaries, and the varying responses he evoked.

The portraits given by Matthew, Mark, Luke and John were based either on personal recollections, or on what they had learned from others who had lived and worked closely with Jesus. How intimate is the story they tell of the kindest of friends who was betrayed by a friend for thirty pieces of silver, of the utterly self-effacing Galilean carpenter who is the Lord of history and the Light of the World.

The Gospel writers believed in the full 'humanity' of Jesus, but they found they could not confine their thinking about him within the meaning of that word. In an attempt to express something of the wonder and grandeur, the mystery and meaning of Jesus, whom God had raised from the dead, they used such phrases as 'the Son of God' and 'the Word of God'. In so doing they did not pretend to be theological professors. Far from it. They were simple, practical men struggling to express in simple terms who Jesus was, and what had been the nature of his mission and work. They were, as Martin Luther said, 'like little children learning to speak, who can speak only in half-words or quarter words'. Though no words were adequate, yet words had to be found to express what they felt about one who was truly unique.

In the early part of the twentieth century Albert Schweitzer did a survey of every important nineteenth century Life of Jesus. His conclusion was that these biographies tell us much about their authors, but little about Jesus. 'There is no historical task which so reveals a man's true self as the writing of a life of Jesus.' The temptation is strong to portray Jesus as we would like him to be, conveniently to forget those aspects of his life and teaching which do not fit our preconceived notions and to concentrate on those thoughts and characteristics which are acceptable in our day. Through the whole history of the Church, Jesus has been misrepresented time and time again. Theologians and artists have imparted to his portrait something of the spirit of their own age. European existentialists earlier this century made him a second Socrates. In *The Man Nobody Knows* Bruce Barton highlighted

Jesus' executive qualities as a business man—because he himself was such a business man. America's Moral Majority think of him as a patriotic American. Whereas those of a timid nature portray him as 'gentle, meek and mild', some liberation theologians portray him as supporting armed resistance.

The way we refashion Jesus in our own cherished image, is clearly seen in S. G. F. Brandon's book, *Jesus and the Zealots.* The author, who admits his admiration for guerrilla warfare against imperial powers, portrays Jesus as a stormy revolutionary who regards violence as a justified method of achieving a justified end. Brandon's Jesus is scarcely distinguishable from the Zealots who were in fact first century guerrillas opposed to the overlordship of Rome. Brandon regards the pacifist and anti-nationalist elements in the Gospel tradition as later additions by the Church to the Gospel records, deliberately included to gain greater toleration by proving to the authorities that the Church was not a threat to Rome.

Some argue that the Gospel writers were also guilty in this respect, that in their writings they reveal as much of themselves and of their own times as they do of Jesus, that the Jesus they portray bears little resemblance to the real Jesus of history. I do not accept this. It is certainly true that the Gospels, like most histories and biographies, were written to plead a cause and to bear witness to beliefs that the writers deemed important. But the fact that they are a combination of report and testimony, that the story is told from the standpoint of faith in the Risen Christ, does not, I believe, invalidate the essential historical reliability of the overall portrait they provide of Jesus. Had it been the writers' intention to extol Jesus by investing him with those qualities and powers which characterised the heroes of popular belief, they would not have written so candidly of his weariness, thirst, weeping and agony. Would they not have been tempted to represent him as being more in accord with contemporary expectations of what the Messiah would be like— a figure of great power, splendour and majesty, one who would

re-establish Jewish political independence and economic pros-
perity? Would they not also have portrayed him as being more
orthodox with respect to the sacred Jewish law?

The cruel taunts levelled against Jesus by his enemies are, I
believe, further evidence that the Gospels not only bear witness
to what the early Church believed about Jesus, but can be
accepted as essentially trustworthy evidence about the historic
Jesus. How they flung mud. 'Look at the company he keeps. He
mixes with publicans, loose women and criminals'; the implication being 'birds of a feather . . . .' Resenting his obvious power
to heal, the Jewish leaders obtusely said that he had been given it
by Satan with whom he was obviously in league. Even as he
hung on the Cross, his strength growing weaker, they continued
with their taunts: 'He saved others, but He cannot save himself'.[1]
Even though they hated him, they could not deny he had
helped, healed and saved many. However sceptical some may be
concerning the reliability of what Jesus' friends said about him,
few doubt the authenticity of such cruel taunts as 'He is a
blasphemer',[2] 'He is mad',[3] 'Look at him, a glutton and a
drinker'.[4] These are not the kind of remarks that friends, wanting
to commend him, would have invented.

Although the response of the Jewish leaders, who heard Jesus
with their own ears and saw him with their own eyes, differed
markedly from that of the Gospel writers, yet the composite
portrait we get of Jesus starting from the criticisms of his
enemies—that of a man who loved the good things of life, a
brilliant teacher who made staggering claims for himself, who
befriended the drop-outs and untouchables, who had a bias
towards the poor, who was on the side of health against sickness,
brotherhood against prejudice—is similar to the overall picture
given by those who gave up home and livelihood to follow him. I
find it remarkable how much of what his enemies said to malign
him, unwittingly justified him, and how many of their slan-
derous remarks contained great compliments and insights.

The comments made by the 'uncommitted', those who would

have argued they were neither for or against Jesus, are also precious testimony to the essential accuracy of the portraits given by his friends. Had there not been something very striking about Jesus, would Jewish observers have likened him to Elijah,[5] one of the greatest of all the Jewish prophets, a man with fire in his bones? Or would the Roman centurion have marvelled at his authority?[6] Would Pilate, who unwittingly became the first person to write about Jesus as king, have been so impressed?[7]

Emerson said of Jesus, 'His name is not so much written, as ploughed into the history of the world'. By studying what casual observers and his enemies said of him, as well as what his friends said, I hope that some might reach a more balanced understanding of history's supreme personality, and better comprehend not only the 'why' of his power to attract and repel, but also *who* he really is.

Notes and References

1   Mark 15:31
2   Matthew 26:65
3   John 10:20
4   Luke 7:34
5   Mark 8:28
6   Matthew 8:5f
7   John 19:19

1

The Madman

When someone is described as crazy or mad, what is said may be true. His reason may be disordered. He may be living in an unreal world. But the verdict could also reveal a great deal about the person who reached such a conclusion. When Galileo first taught that the earth moved, people said he was deranged. But years later his teaching was seen to be the product of a penetrating mind. Today we suspect the sanity of anyone who denies this. St Francis' contemporaries were sure he was a fool to leave a rich merchant's home to care for the poor and the lepers. The fact that he wrote 'hit' songs in which birds thanked God for the air that supported them, and the sun and the moon praised God for creating them, further convinced them that he was out of his mind, and yet the historians acknowledge that this 'holy fool' was one of the most significant people in the thirteenth century. He, probably more than anyone else, was responsible for bringing the Church out of the Dark Ages, and renewing the faith of the centuries that followed. How tempting it is for us to regard as crazy those who think and behave differently, who value things by other standards, who refuse to spend money on what we think matters a great deal, who regard as important things we deem unimportant.

In the field of engineering a crank is 'a piece of technology that creates revolutions'. I find it significant that often in the history of the world it has been the so-called 'cranks' who have inspired the most beneficial revolutions. Today the Jewish prophets are classed with the greatest thinkers of all time, yet in the eyes of their contemporaries they were thought to be cranks. Jonathan Swift, the Dean of St Patrick's Cathedral in Dublin, and the author of *Gulliver's Travels,* was dismissed by many as mad, for unlike many in the eighteenth century he was deeply stirred by the shame and horror which people inflict on one another in the name of money, patriotism and religion. It is a sad commentary on human nature that Swift's hatred of slavery, war and poverty, should have caused him to be regarded as both crazy and unpatriotic. In 1959 Kruschev said of the USSR, 'We have no opponents of our system. Only a few madmen'. Pasternak, Solzhenitsyn, Sakharov—madmen? I doubt if that will be the verdict of history.

It was no different in Jesus' day. Behind his magnetic personality and busy round of helpful activity, were certain powerfully-held convictions. These were the source of his great public influence. They were also the cause of his early death. People do not crucify a do-gooder, no matter how misguided they think he is. The Pharisees plotted Jesus' death because each time they came into contact with him, they were confronted with a set of convictions which threatened much that they held dear. Some resorted to the simple conclusion: 'He is mad'[1] and 'out of his mind'.[2]

Now, by Pharisaic standards, Jesus' behaviour was irregular and his intellect disordered. He turned the hierarchy of human values upside down. Who but a madman would have taught that God loves bad people as well as good, Samaritans and Romans as well as Jews; that folk with one talent are as important to God as people with ten; that the really important things in life are simple acts of service, like giving a cup of cold water to a thirsty man, or visiting someone in prison? Who but a madman would have talked of admitting riff-raff to the royal banquet, or of 'not being anxious what we shall eat or drink or wear',[3] or of being good to them that hate us, or of the meek inheriting the earth? In dismissing Jesus as deranged, the Pharisees felt certain that they were setting the world to right once more.

Where did sanity lie, with the Pharisees or with Jesus? We have to choose. Their moral values and religious outlooks were so radically different. Jesus regarded human need as more important than Sabbath regulations; justice and compassion as having priority over religious etiquette. 'You pay tithes of mint and rue and every garden herb, but have no care for justice and the love of God. It is these you should have practised without neglecting the others.'[4] Jesus put integrity above reputation. He regarded the advancement of God's Kingdom as more important than his own advancement.

Where does sanity lie today? I have no doubt as to the answer. Jesus has been described as the Messiah, the Son of God, the Son of Man. He could also be called with justification, 'The Master Mind' of the centuries. This aspect of Jesus' supremacy has I believe, received too little emphasis. Yet it is here I find his supremacy most clear. With the passing centuries the convictions Jesus implanted in the world's mind have become more relevant, not less:

The beatitudes are beautiful attitudes.
'Blessed are the merciful, the peace-makers, those who hunger and thirst after righteousness . . . .'[5]
What we are is of greater significance than what we own or what we wear.
Greatness does not consist in having many servants, but in being a servant.
There is a glory about going the second mile and doing the bit over.
Every day is holy, every act of service a sacred thing.
Mankind is one family—all men and women are God's children.
Happiness comes more through giving than getting.
We find ourselves by responding to the challenges and demands of life, not by avoiding them.

Here was a mind that saw truly. The passing of time and the ripening of experience has driven me to the conclusion that the controlling convictions of Jesus' mind are the most important convictions for all human beings in all times. Arthur Compton, a Nobel prize-winning physicist, underlined the wisdom of 'loving our neighbours as we love ourselves', when he said, 'In our effort to attain the beautiful and the good, we find that now to a greater degree this can best be done when we endeavour to attain these same objectives for others as well as ourselves'.

'You have learned that they were told, "Eye for eye, tooth for tooth". But what I tell you is this. Do not set yourself against the man who wrongs you. . . . Love your enemies and pray for your persecutors.'[6] The more common such sense becomes, the better for the human race. What is happening today in the Middle East and Northern Ireland is a powerful reminder that vengeance never evens the score. It ties both the injured and the injurer to an endless escalation of retaliation. Forgiveness on the other hand breaks the vicious chain reaction.

In his book *The Night of the New Moon,* Laurens van der Post speaks of his experiences in a Japanese prisoner of war camp during the Second World War.

> I came out of prison longing passionately that the past would be recognised as past before it could spread another form of putrefaction in the spirit of our time. My prison experience had taught me that forgiveness is as fundamental a law of the human spirit as the law of gravity. If one broke the law of forgiveness, one inflicted a mortal wound on one's spirit and became once again a member of a chain gang of mere cause and effect.[7]

He tells later how, as he watched the War Crimes investigators being 'more bitter and vengeful about our suffering than we were ourselves . . . [he] learned to fear the Pharisee more than the sinner'.

In Bernard Shaw's play *St Joan,* one of the characters complains to Poulengay, 'You are as mad as the Maid is'. He replies, 'We want a few mad people now. See where the sane ones have landed us'. What passes for normality in modern life has produced a great deal of callousness, bitterness and cynicism. For instance, many hearts have been hardened and families destroyed over the contents of wills. Thackeray told of two sisters who clung to each other until they quarrelled over a £20 legacy. Thereafter they never spoke. Is that not madness? Are we not foolish to have allowed things acquired to become *the* symbol of success, *the* index of superiority? Are we not crazy to pass on ourselves the awful sentence: 'to attain, to advance, to acquire until death do us part'? One of the ironies of our time is that selfish, grasping, insensitive business men and women are considered normal and well-adjusted. Jesus called them 'fools'.[8] It concerned him that many, like Dives, were content to live in their own private little world, preoccupied only with the feathering of their own nest, and the building up of their own reputation. Some years ago a novel was written about life in a mental hospital. The title *Private Worlds,* highlighted the fact that the unfortunate people being cared for were living in a little private world of their own feelings and fancies, out of touch with real life. But is that not true of millions who have never been certified? They live in their own private universe, insensitive to the appalling needs of others and the big problems of the world. Up to a point, possessions, wealth and promotion can liberate, but once a certain stage is reached we have to be on our guard lest they clog our lives and distort our vision of what really matters.

Many today are convinced that the mediaeval monks were crazy to punish their bodies in the way they did. And yet I wonder if any monk ever inflicted as much punishment on his body, heart or nervous system, as do many modern go-getters. Diseases like the ulcer, thrombosis and nervous breakdown have become in our day like the plague in the Middle Ages, just part of the everyday face of things. Many are too busy with making a living to live, too hurried and worried to see and smell and touch. It really is a kind of madness that has taken hold of us, a madness that demands that in order to be business and social successes, we must often be failures as human beings and parents, with little or no time to love or be loved by family and neighbours.

The questions which Jesus addressed to his contemporaries, and the way of life he advocated, are as relevant today as in his own day. 'What does a man gain by winning the whole world at the cost of his true self?'[9] 'Even when a man has more than enough, his wealth does not give him life.'[10] 'Anyone who wishes to be a follower of mine, must leave self behind.'[11]

Gérard de Nerval once described Jesus as the 'madman, incredibly sublime'. That is not a bad description. Long ago Paul wrote to the Christians at Corinth: 'We are fools for Christ's sake, while you are such sensible Christians. We are weak; you are so powerful. We are in disgrace, you are honoured. They curse us and we bless . . . .'[12]

If to be sane is to be like our modern world, and if to be mad is to be Christ-like, then perhaps 'sublime insanity' is our greatest need.

Notes and References

1   John 10:20
2   Mark 3:21
3   Matthew 6:31
4   Luke 11:42
5   Matthew 5:3–10
6   Matthew 5:38,39,43,44
7   pp 121–124
8   Luke 12:20
9   Mark 8:36
10   Luke 12:15
11   Mark 8:34
12   1 Corinthians 4:10

2

The Man for God

From time to time it has been suggested that Jesus and Christianity appeal only to a certain kind of person. In the second century a Roman called Celsus tried to make out that the appeal of Jesus was only to the lower strata of society, the common uneducated mob. In the nineteenth century Sigmund Freud believed that Christianity appealed only to the gullible. Earlier this century Hitler maintained that Jesus appealed only to the cowardly and the effeminate. But any honest analysis of the biblical and historical facts would quickly disprove such suggestions.

John records how Greeks as well as Jews came to Philip and said, 'Sir we should like to see Jesus'.[1] He tells how on another occasion the Pharisees said to one another, 'All the world has gone after him'.[2] 'The world', people of all classes and ages, not just poor farmers and illiterate shepherds, not just Jewish women and children, but people of wealth and learning, people of different national and religious backgrounds, all going after a village carpenter who did not count socially.

The appeal of Jesus was to the up and in as well as the down and out. His friendship recreated in many dubious characters a belief in goodness long lost. People of higher moral standards were also attracted. Nicodemus was a high-ranking Pharisee. What his fellow-Pharisees might think, his own position in Jerusalem; these pulled one way, but Jesus pulled the other. Visiting under cover of night, Nicodemus addressed Jesus with the utmost respect: 'We know you are a teacher sent by God'.[3] The fact that Jesus was such an exciting individual that fishermen left their nets and homes to follow him, that a rich young man ran to learn his secret, that many Jews were putting 'their faith

in him',[4] so upset the Pharisees that they convened a meeting of
the Sanhedrin to see what action they should take. John tells
how one speaker said, 'If we leave him alone like this, the whole
populace will believe in him'.[5]

Whereas the simplicity of Jesus' life and teaching has en-
thralled many a lowly soul, the profundity of his words and
personality has captivated intellectual giants, like Paul, Augus-
tine, Aquinas, Dostoevsky, Schweitzer and Solzhenitsyn.
Common folk in every age have loved him, so too have many of
royal lineage like Columba, Saint Mungo and Queen Margaret.[6]
Men of action like Edward Wilson of the Antarctic and David
Livingstone; artistic and musical geniuses like Michelangelo and
Bach, were also attracted. When the Jewish parents of Bruno
Walter expressed their amazement at their son's attraction to the
Christian faith, Bruno replied, 'Jesus Christ, how could I not
love him?'[7]

A film critic wrote concerning the film, 'The King of Kings':
'I stood at the door of the cinema and watched the people coming
in, joking and laughing like any other crowd of amusement
seekers; and three hours later I saw them come out, silent and
thoughtful, awed and subdued, with a look of wonder and
wistful inquiry in their tear-stained eyes'. What is it about Jesus
that exercises this appeal? What was it about him in his own day
that compelled the reverent respect, not only of many Jews but
also of thoughtful Greeks and Romans? Was it his outstanding
ability as teacher or preacher, or his sincerity and courage?
Perhaps these were part of the attraction, though it should be
remembered that the Greek nation was renowned for its orators
and teachers. Sincerity and courage were also common virtues in
the ancient world. I believe the real attraction of Jesus stemmed
from other characteristics which were more distinct in his day.

God was real to Jesus. For Jesus, the existence and the love of
God, far from being interesting ideas to theorise and argue
about, were the most certain facts in the world, the inspiration
of his every thought, word and deed. Jesus lived and died, not to

draw attention to himself, but to reveal that at the heart of all things, love reigns and heaven cares.

To speak of Jesus as though for him 'God-language' was no part of his life and ministry, as some scholars have done, is to betray genuine historical perspective. Though Jesus was, as existentialist theologians have said, 'the Man for Others', and though he was (as liberation theologians have pointed out) the 'uniquely free Man', yet first and foremost he was the 'Man for God'.

Jesus prayed to God in the intimate way a person would speak to his own father. In his teaching he kept directing people's thoughts away from himself to One whom he knew to be a loving Father. His parables all view life from the divine perspective. With his last breath he committed himself to God's care. However meaningless the concept of God may be for some today, it was certainly not so for Jesus.

His power to heal was also distinctive. More than half the recorded acts of Jesus have to do with healing. The Roman centurion was so impressed by the healing energies apparently at his disposal, that he said, 'Say the word and my servant will be cured'.[8] A timorous woman was equally sure she would be healed if she could but touch the hem of his cloak.[9] He went about healing all manner of sickness and disease, not for self-glory, nor to gain followers, but because he genuinely cared for people.

Because people trusted and believed in him, his words were able to get past their critical faculties into the depths of the sub-conscious, to those hidden doubts, anxieties and conflicts which are so often the root of the trouble. Jesus conceived health in terms of wholeness, the proper functioning of body, mind and spirit. Many were healed because Jesus gave them a changed way of looking at things and people, a changed way of looking at themselves and God. His was a message with healing implications. Jesus did not claim to heal every disease. But he knew what psychosomatic medicine accepts as fact, that many of the ailments from which people suffer, stem from the 'dis-ease' of man with himself, and his hidden conflicts in the close relationships that make up his life. An African tribe has an alternative phrase for worry. They say 'My mind is killing me'. What a telling phrase that is. Doctors rightly ask on occasions, '*Who* is the matter with you?' rather than '*What* is the matter with you?'

At other times people speak of being sick of themselves. Jesus knew that such sickness often stems from man's broken relationship with God. When healing takes place at this deep level, physical healing often follows. Even when bodily weakness remains, people are yet made 'whole', or 'healthy' in the truest sense.

The universality of Jesus' love was another distinctive characteristic. Jesus mixed freely with the poor, the prostitutes, the ritually unclean. He went where need called, regardless of his own reputation. In the eyes of the official representatives of Judaism, he was tactless, incautious and lacking discernment. He had no sense of the right contacts.[10] With delicious irony, Jesus replied that the religious leaders were so respectably righteous that they did not need a doctor, but that the poor, the outcast and those less respectable, did![11]

The concern of Jesus for the foreigner also contrasted sharply, not only with the disdainful Jewish outlook, but also with the Gentile. To the Greeks the very name for foreigner was the same as that for barbarian. Jesus on the other hand, in thought and outlook, was so much a citizen of the world, that many today do not think of him as a Jew.

There was also a *greater intensity* about Christ's love. For the Stoics the ideal state was 'apathy': 'Teach yourself not to care lest you get hurt'. But Jesus said in effect, 'Care passionately even though you get hurt'. To try to describe the amazing compassion which Jesus had for friend and foe, for the socially unacceptable as well as the socially acceptable, the New Testament writers brought into prominence a classical Greek word which was seldom used—*agape*. They reminted it to describe Christ's extravagant love. Few doubt it was Jesus who sat in the studio of Paul's imagination when he wrote, 'Love is patient; love is kind and envies no one. Love is never boastful nor conceited, nor rude; never selfish, not quick to take offence. Love keeps no score of wrongs; does not gloat over other men's sins, but delights in the truth'.[12]

There was also the stress which Jesus laid on *forgiveness*. This was probably the most distinct innovation that Jesus made in morality. Today when a Christian spirit is spoken of, a forgiving spirit is usually meant. In the pre-Christian world, life was a matter of getting even when wronged, of hitting back, of dog eat dog. Jesus taught a nobler way. Aware that hate and violence multiply in a chain reaction of destruction, Jesus forgave the person who wronged him. He kept no wrongs green. Even when spat upon and crucified, he prayed, 'Father forgive them, they know not what they do'.[13] As an old man, Peter could still not get over the wonder of how when Jesus 'was abused he did not retort with abuse'.[14]

Jesus' humility was also distinctive. Whereas his contemporaries thought of greatness in terms of wealth, power and cleverness, Jesus thought of it in terms of service to others. Without any pose he took a towel, girded himself and washed his disciples' feet. Whereas those on top in the ancient world looked for thrones to sit on, Jesus 'humbled himself and in obedience accepted even death on a cross'.[15]

Humility as Jesus understood it, does not mean 'hating the limelight' or avoiding all fiercely contested areas of controversy. In his dealings with the Jewish leaders, Jesus showed a confidence that had no trace of inferiority; his humility was humility before God. He kept reminding his hearers that his talents, power and teaching came from God. We speak of people being 'gifted', but lacking Jesus' humility seldom ask 'gifted by whom?' or 'gifted for what?' So conscious was Jesus of God, that he was completely free from the self-consciousness which often spoils humility. Worn outwardly, as with Uriah Heep, humility is offensive to God and man.

And the devil did grin
For his darling sin
Is the pride that apes humility.

Though people may be impure, proud, unloving and unforgiving, and though God may not be real to them, there is something in most of them that responds to genuine humility, to caring, forgiving love and vital faith. There *is* a universal appeal about Jesus and what is Christ-like.

Notes and References

1 John 12:21
2 John 12:19
3 John 3:1
4 John 11:45
5 John 11:48
6 In addition to her other queenly duties, Margaret fed and cared for orphans. She also served 2000 poor people regularly in the palace dining hall.
7 BBC TV programme on Bruno Walter, 1972
8 Luke 7:7
9 Matthew 9:20
10 See further—Chapters 10 and 12
11 Mark 2:17
12 1 Corinthians 13:4f
13 Luke 23:34
14 1 Peter 2:23
15 Philippians 2:8

3

The Troublemaker

In the shadow of Mount Hermon, when Jesus asked his disciples, 'What are men saying about me?', he was told, 'Some say you are John the Baptist'.[1]

When Herod, the killer of John, was informed of the doings and sayings of Jesus, in an anguish of superstitious fear, he cried out, 'This is John whom I beheaded raised from the dead'.[2] How strange this comparison seems. The initial impression is that Jesus and John the Baptist were as far apart as the austerity of winter from the warmth of summer. Was not John the Baptist a 'loner', an unkempt ascetic who lived in the desert, an old-time 'hell-fire-and-brimstone' preacher? Jesus on the other hand sat at people's tables and shared their conversation. He feasted while John fasted. Whereas John proclaimed the wrath of God and pending doom, Jesus kept stressing God's love and his willingness to forgive. Whereas the crowds went out into the wilderness to hear John, Jesus went into the towns and villages where the crowds already were.

Jesus once contrasted John's ministry and his own in a vivid metaphor. John's ministry is like a funeral, mine like a wedding.[3] With such marked differences there must undoubtedly have been striking similarities, otherwise people would never have likened Jesus to John. What were these similarities?

Both were men of deep conviction. 'Sent from God',[4] they lived their lives, not in conformity to the dictates of society, but in obedience to God. Both talked in a very human way about everyday things, like giving a shirt away if you have two, and sharing food with the hungry. They both had tremendous compassion for the victims of this world, for the poor, and those discriminated against. They were a voice for those who had no voice. Both spoke of the need to repent[5], the need for a change of heart. Of John the Baptist, Josephus said, 'He was a good man who commended the Jews to practise virtue, and to be just to one another and devout towards God'. That was true also of Jesus.

The likening of Jesus to John reminds us that the prettified, haloed image, pseudo-feminine (but unworthy of woman), which many have of the founder of Christianity, is the product of weak thinking and Christian bad taste. What a misrepresentation of the Gospels!

Harvey Cox writes, 'My favourite work of art is the mural by José Clemente Orozco, the Mexican painter, showing the Risen Christ with a huge axe felling the cross on a heap of symbols of the world's cruelty, avarice and hatred. It is a brilliant reminder that the sweet gentle Jesus we so much adore . . . has another side'.[6] A namby-pamby, unheroic figure would never have been likened to John, who radiated vitality and courage. John was no 'reed shaken by the wind'.[7] He was not putty to be squeezed into any shape. He openly and fearlessly denounced the irregular marriage of Herod. It might cost him his life—in fact it did—but he was not deterred. 'You have no right to your brother's wife.'[8] God's law had been broken. Outraged also by the moral slackness of his day, John accepted the consequences of reminding the royal court and the ruling classes that they were breaking the moral law. The fact that he might be judged intolerant and narrow-minded did not silence him. He rebuked the tax-collectors for over-charging, the Roman soldiers for bullying.

When circumstances demanded it, there was a cutting edge to Jesus' teaching also. Although it was in words of heart-breaking tenderness that Jesus expressed his love for the city which was to murder him, and his compassion for all who were weary and heavy-laden, these were far from being the only words he uttered. His words often crackled with the fire of his prophetic forebears. The Jewish leaders were upset because like John the Baptist, Jesus 'paid deference to no one'.[9] His anger blazed against their abuse of power and influence, their exploitation of the weak and helpless. 'Alas for you lawyers and Pharisees . . . outside you look like honest men, but inside you are brimful of hypocrisy and crime.' [10] He openly denounced pride and selfishness, especially when he saw them parading under the guise of religion. He charged the Pharisees and Sadducees with being 'blind guides', [11] and 'savage wolves'. [12] He lashed out at Pharisees who sanctified everything that was traditional, smothering the human spirit in unquestioning worship of the past. His uncompromising remarks about their stuffy unexamined piety, and their bigoted nit-picking, put him at odds with the Jewish leaders. They were certainly not the kind to 'win friends and influence people'. The fact that Jesus, like John, was a troublemaker, may be embarrassing, but it is true. Both made trouble, not for their own sake or for trouble's sake, but for God's sake.

The impression we get of Jesus from the Gospels is of a man of unflinching courage. 'Courage,' as Sir Edmond Hilary said, 'often means being afraid, and yet carrying on as though you do not know what fear is.' With what steel-like determination Jesus set out on his last journey to Jerusalem and certain death. An itinerant preacher against entrenched religion, a prophet taking on the might of the Jewish hierarchy, a poor man tangling with privileged wealth. You cannot get anything more dramatic than that.

Jesus did not have, to use the glib cliché, a death wish. But neither was he willing to stand by and watch the temple being desecrated and people being short-changed. A house of prayer had been turned into a cattle-market, a bazaar, a great money-making machine. He got into trouble, not because he said, 'Consider the lilies in the field, how they grow', but because he said, 'Consider the thieves in the temple, how they steal'.

Jesus must often have been tempted to compromise, to remain silent. There were times when his own friends tried to get him to be more tactful. 'It is easy to be brave when all behind agree with you, but the trouble comes when ninety-nine of your friends think you are wrong. Then it is a brave soul who stands up . . . remembering that one on God's side is a majority.'[13] Jesus spoke out bravely on live issues, which, then as now, are nearly always controversial. Like John he refused to tamper with truth, or to temper his message to make it congenial to his hearers. Peter's earnest plea that Jesus should make a few compromises for pity's sake, was to no avail. Jesus refused to trim his sails to changing winds of popularity. 'He taught in all honesty the way of life God requires.'[14]

A satirical book on how to be popular as a preacher gives the following advice. 'Never be specific as to the Christian position on any burning social issues . . . preach on the problems that are as remote as possible from your own community. You can denounce the government of South Africa with all the vigour at your command, but be careful about denouncing political corruption in your own city, because some of your own good members might be involved. Keep handy a set of non-specific words and phrases which allow the members of the congregation to fill in their own meaning . . . brotherhood, Christian love. . . .'[15]

Jesus did not tactfully avoid burning issues. He knew that tact in itself is no virtue, that there is hardly any kind of compromise which cannot be disguised as tact even from oneself. When he first preached in the synagogue in Nazareth, with his family all gathered, listening intently and privately hoping he would not expound any of his new-fangled ideas, what did he do but raise those very issues and awkward questions which they felt he should have left alone. Truth often being like light to sore eyes, small wonder the congregation became an angry protesting mob.[16]

Jesus did not conceal from his disciples the risks which would be involved in making plain and public their Christian convictions. He knew the moral demands of discipleship often outweigh the intellectual. 'Woe unto you when all men shall speak well of you.'[17] The soft purring of universal approval can mean a person has made so complete an adjustment to this world's outlook that he no longer counts as a saving force in it. The Church has all too often set up a false choice—either to be prophets or lovers. Jesus called on his followers to be both.

Notes and References

1   Mark 8:28
2   Mark 6:16
3   Matthew 11:16
4   John 1:6
5   See next Chapter
6   A. D. Magazine, April 1974
7   Matthew 11:7
8   Mark 6:18
9   Luke 20:21
10 Matthew 23:13,28
11 Matthew 23:16
12 Matthew 7:15
13 Wendell Phillips
14 Luke 20:21
15 *How to become a bishop without being religious.* Charles M. Smith
16 Luke 4:21-30
17 Luke 6:26

4

A Mighty Prophet

'Who do men say that I am?', asked Jesus. 'Some say John the Baptist, others Elijah, others one of the prophets.'[1] The thought that Jesus might possibly be a prophet had even occurred to Simon the Pharisee. 'If this man were a prophet. . . .'[2] That some of his contemporaries should liken Jesus to the prophets, and especially to Elijah, is again indicative of the deep impression Jesus was making. It is not easy to exaggerate the eminent place Elijah occupied in the minds of orthodox Jews. Many believed he would reappear before God's kingdom would come in power.[3] For centuries orthodox Jews had been longing for his return, their hearts at times almost sick with waiting. On the occasion of the great Jewish festivals, some set a vacant place for Elijah at their supper table.

There are people who deplore the miraculous in the stories of Elijah; but if we are to catch glimpses of this man of God as his own people saw him, we must not so rapidly dispose of the miraculous. In vivid language we are told of the angel bringing food to the tired man, of Elijah parting the waters with his mantle, of God revealing himself to the prophet in the wind, fire and earthquake, and of the chariots and horses of fire which finally carried Elijah from human sight. Such impressive language and imagery were used by oriental artists, who were not cursed with our literal minds, to portray a reality which might otherwise escape their readers. They felt that only in this way could the stature of this man and his significance for his own day be adequately recorded and communicated. Only in this way could they show that here had been a fearless man of God. In defiance of a despotic and ruthless queen he had won back the hearts of his faithless people, and had restored the sacred altar of

Jehovah that Jezebel would have destroyed. Here indeed was a giant of the faith. In an attempt to do justice to his greatness, the writer of the Book of Kings splashes his brush across the canvas.

Even if all we knew of Jesus was that some who came into close contact with him whispered to their neighbours, 'Is this Elijah?', we could safely deduce that they ranked this Galilean carpenter very highly. Otherwise they would not have thought to put him on a par with the hero of Mount Carmel.

'Who do men say that I am?' 'Some say Elijah—others one of the prophets.' The description of Jesus as a prophet occurs often in the New Testament. The Palm Sunday crowd referred to him as 'the prophet Jesus from Nazareth'.[4] On another occasion his contemporaries said, 'A great prophet has arisen among us'.[5] This was a real tribute, for the prophets were the most extra-ordinary phenomenon in the history of Israel. They filled the role occupied in Western civilisation by poet, historian, novelist and orator.

A striking characteristic of the Hebrew prophets was the way they brought divine insight to bear on the injustices and the problems of the societies in which they lived, the way they kept reminding their contemporaries and those in authority of God's ways in the past, and His demands for the present. The prophets were no 'armchair' or 'grandstand' philosophers of history. They were absorbed in the issues of their time. They knew what was going on in the corrupt corridors of power, the rack-rented slums, the debtors' prisons and the geriatric wards of their day. They were critical of religious ritual and ceremonial laws which bore no relation to righteousness. They were also critical of a Sabbath which bore little relation to the other six days. 'I hate, I spurn your pilgrim-feasts; I will not delight in your sacred ceremonies. . . . Let justice roll on like a river and righteousness like an ever-flowing stream.'[6] When praying, the Jews used to lift their hands on high. Isaiah went so far as to tell heartless worshippers that what God saw was the blood of the oppressed dripping from their fingers. What use, the prophets asked, is religious ritual if it does not make people more caring?

This was still a problem in the time of Jesus. Religious observance often had precious little to do with loving God or one's neighbour. Jesus knew people who went to the synagogue every Sabbath, and to the Jerusalem temple every year, and came home more narrow-minded, prejudiced and indifferent than before.

It is little wonder Jesus' contemporaries thought of him as a prophet, for much that he taught was in the prophetic tradition. He offered consolation to the poor. He strongly condemned unjust rulers and the unconcerned rich. For Jesus, as for the prophets, justice and mercy had priority over animal sacrifice. He censured the priest and Levite for passing by human need on the other side, for thinking their professional schedules and religious systems mattered more than human beings.

It is a pity that many today think of the Jewish prophets merely as eccentric seers, as fore-tellers of the future, for with the greatest of the Old Testament prophets the element of prediction was incidental rather than essential. The doctor who diagnoses cancer or sclerosis, can often tell with considerable accuracy the future health pattern of his patient. The trained marriage counsellor or social worker often recognises signs of friction and differences of opinion, which if persisted in will finally lead to the break-up of the home. Likewise, the prophets, seeing how far their fellow-Jews had wandered from God's laws and God's ways, how they had betrayed their high destiny, clearly foretold the tragic consequences. They were men of profound insight rather than second-sight. Elijah, Amos, Hosea, Isaiah, Jeremiah, dissociated themselves from the fortune-tellers of their day. When they spoke of the future it was in the light of their understanding of the relationship which ought to exist between man and God and of their deep faith that ultimately righteousness exalts the life of a nation, while selfishness and immorality degrade. 'Like delicate seismograph instruments, they sensed the far-off tremors of coming earthquakes.'[7]

The prophets were on the side of the poor, the hungry, the underdogs and the ill-treated. They were outraged when they saw people discriminated against or exploited. Jesus was also implacably opposed to corruption, avarice, injustice and oppression. His manifesto was a quotation from the prophet Isaiah:

> The spirit of the Lord is upon me, because he has anointed me;
> he has sent me to announce good news to the poor,
> to proclaim release for prisoners and recovery of sight for the blind;
> to let the broken victims go free.[8]

Jesus' prime concern was not with some special kind of monastic life, or life hereafter, but life in this world, life spelled out in social, economic and political relationships.

Some would disagree. They maintain that Jesus' teaching was not intended for this world, but for the divine society yet to come, when Christ will reign in glory, when heaven will come to earth. But is this not mistaken? 'Pray for your persecutors.'[9] Will there be persecutors in the millenium? Whoever 'makes you to go a mile, go with him two'.[10] Will there be bullies in heaven pushing people around? Like the prophets, Jesus' ethical teaching was concerned with how people should live in this world. He came not primarily to get us into heaven, but to get more of heaven into us and our society.

In the 1930s Martin Niemoller went to Hitler and told him of his concern for the future of the German nation. 'Let that be my concern,' replied Hitler. Goebbels said much the same: 'Churchmen dabbling in politics should take note that their only task is to prepare people for the world hereafter'. That was not how the Jewish prophet or Jesus conceived their mission. Salvation for them was not simply a matter of the soul, but of the whole person.

The Book of Amos is short. Dynamite usually comes in small packages! What Amos said about the exploitation of the poor, about lack of adequate social services for those in trouble, about greedy loan sharks and corrupt law courts, was so explosive that he was asked to leave Bethel. It is little different 2500 years later. A South American bishop says, 'If I give bread to the poor they call me a saint; but if I ask "Why is there so little bread for the poor?", they arrest me and charge me with being a communist'. Jesus and the prophets were concerned that the hungry should be fed, the naked clothed, and widows and orphans supported and housed. They were concerned to establish an order of society which would reflect the righteousness of God and His concern for the defenceless and the oppressed. Yet they also knew that all schemes for a better and fairer world are at best half-schemes, unless accompanied by a change in the human heart.

It is a great pity that 'repentance' has today become an embarrassing word, for it is central to the message of the prophets and Jesus. The biblical writers taught that what had gone wrong with the human situation was that people, having asserted their independence of God, had each made themselves the centre of their own world. Self-centred they had become self-assertive. They had fought strenuously to extend their own little empires with little or no thought either for God or other people. In a land where many lived below the poverty line, the rich fool's main concern was where to store his excess grain.[11]

The prophets and Jesus sought to change people's relationship to God and to one another. Though genuinely concerned that the hungry should be fed, and that the poor should have better living conditions, yet they knew that changing tax-laws, wages and housing policies would not of themselves usher in the millennium. Jesus knew he had failed in towns like Capernaum, Bethsaida and Chorazin. What was lacking was a change of heart. Popularity was his for the asking there, but not repentance. The inhabitants wanted their problems solved, but not at the price of having their lives fundamentally changed. 'Repent' means 'turn about'. It is a movement in which we shift our position so that we are facing in a different direction—Christ's direction. In a poem by Thomas More, the one who is charged with bringing to heaven the world's greatest treasure finally comes with a tear of repentance. That is a thoroughly biblical concept. Jesus spoke often of the rejoicing there was in heaven when a person turns from the way which leads *from* the Kingdom of Heaven into the way that leads *to* it.

In the time of the Jewish prophets, as in New Testament times, there were strong anti-monarchist and anti-Roman feelings. There were also strong antipathies on the part of the poor to the upper classes. Though Jesus and the prophets were on the side of the underdog and those unjustly treated, they never tried violently to wrench power or wealth from the hands of the strong and the rich. They were aware how violent revolution often results in the labels being changed, but not the evil and injustice. The origin of the word 'revolution' illustrates its inherent weakness. It is a term borrowed from astronomy. The planets make their revolutions, but they always come back to where they were. So with human beings. Violent revolutions usually take them back to much the same tyrannies and inequities—only under different dress. Before the shouts of victory die away, the new order begins to display an uncomfortable resemblance to the old. The top people come down and the bottom ones go up—without changing the nature of either. In other cases, swift revolutions have a habit of collapsing in a recoil of hideous reaction. Instead, Jesus and the prophets sought to give people a vision of a world at peace, a world in which they want to be brothers and sisters, sharing and caring, a world where they want to beat swords into ploughshares and spears into pruning hooks.

Some have tried to justify violent revolution by pointing to Jesus' cleansing of the temple. But that was no *coup d'etat*. Even the Jewish leaders knew that. Had they had even the faintest suspicion that it was a take-over bid, they would have sent for the help of the Roman garrison stationed in the castle nearby. God's way of building a better world is one of quiet evolution rather than revolution, the spreading of good people's convictions, the example of brave people's protests. These ultimately make for real progress.

Notes and References

1   Mark 8:28
2   Luke 7:39
3   Mark 9:11
4   Matthew 21:11
5   Luke 7:16
6   Amos 5:21
7   M. E. Macdonald
8   Luke 4:18
9   Matthew 5:44
10   Matthew 5:41
11   Luke 12:15f

A Born Leader

Matthew tells of a company commander in the Roman Army who was distressed about the grave illness of a favourite servant. Approaching Jesus he said, 'You need only say the word and the boy will be cured. I know for I myself am under orders, with soldiers under me. I say to one "Go" and he goes; to another "Come here" and he comes'.[1] The centurion felt that just as he, with the authority of the Roman Emperor behind him, was able to issue orders, so Jesus, who so obviously spoke with the authority of Almighty God, need only say the word and his servant would be cured. What a powerful tribute to the deep impression Jesus made.

Though the records that we have in the Gospels of the call of the disciples are less informative than we might wish, it is quite clear that all twelve left home and livelihood, for the sake of a cause they dimly understood. That they should have responded at all to Jesus' invitation to share his affections and commitments is cause for wonder. There must obviously have been something forceful, authoritative and magnetic about the person of Jesus, for the sacrifices and difficulties involved in leaving home and following him were considerable.

In Galilee, a crowd of several thousand, egged on by members of the Zealot underground movement, wanted Jesus to lead a revolt against the Romans who occupied their beloved land. They obviously felt they were in the presence of a born leader. In the temple at Jerusalem, it was apparently by sheer moral force that Jesus drove the traders from the outer court of the temple.

The same ring of authority characterised Jesus' words. He spoke firmly in the presence of the demented man: 'Be silent (unclean spirit) and come out of him'.[2] 'The tone of voice,' said

G. K. Chesterton, 'reminds one of the tone of a very business-like lion tamer, or a strong-minded doctor dealing with a homicidal maniac.' 'Your sins are forgiven.'[3] Though these words contradicted a basic tenet of Jewish faith, that only God could forgive sins, yet many to whom they were addressed, actually believed Jesus. Nicodemus the Pharisee who sought him out by night, did so because he was convinced there was an eternal dimension to the words and personality of Jesus. 'Rabbi, we know that you are a teacher sent by God.'[4]

Though Jesus had no title, mitre or sceptre, yet his words struck home. The common people 'were astounded at his teaching; unlike their own teachers he taught with a note of authority'.[5] When we say of a teacher, 'He is an authority on his own subject', we mean that we are prepared to accept his judgments in those spheres in which he is knowledgeable. Many of Jesus' contemporaries instinctively felt that he was just such an authority on human nature, faith and life. John tells us, 'He knew men so well, all of them, that he needed no evidence from others about a man, for he himself could tell what was in a man'.[6] His was an inward-seeing love.

Many who heard him teach asked with amazement, how it was that this man, who had no credentials of study or ordination, had such learning. When Jesus replied, 'The teaching that I give is not my own; it is the teaching of him who sent me',[7] again many of the common people believed him. Whereas the Pharisees quoted their authorities, Jesus spoke as one who possessed authority within himself: 'You have learned that our forefathers were told. . . . But what I tell you is this . . . .'[8] Unhesitatingly he pitted his judgment against the long-standing traditions and beliefs of his nation. Without apology he assumed the right to declare what was lawful on the Sabbath, and to dispense with many of the regulations governing fasting and ritual cleansing.

Jesus set before his contemporaries the 'best way of all', hoping that just as light reveals what is shabby and dark, so they would see, by contrast, the inadequacies and falsities of their own way of life. But always Jesus respected people's freedom, even the freedom to betray him. He was prepared to go to great lengths to win back the estranged Judas, but on no account would he resort to force. He gave Judas the honoured seat at the Last Supper and the sop which was normally reserved for the honoured guest, as if to say, 'Judas that is how much I love you. Are you still going to betray me?' But when he saw there was no softening of Judas' heart, he said, 'Do quickly what you have to do'.[9] The obedience which compulsion and legal sanctions produce is a different and inferior thing to the spontaneous loyalty Jesus desired.

Jesus never used the words 'ideal' or 'other-worldly' to describe his teaching, but he did use the adjectives 'wise' and 'sensible'. 'What then of the man who hears these words of mine and acts upon them? He is like a man who had the sense to build his house on rock.'[10] His appeal was far more on the side of sense than sentiment.

Matthew tells us how Jesus met the enquiry as to the authority on which he acted,[11] by the counter question as to whether John the Baptist's authority came from God or man? In doing so he was not seeking to avoid the difficult question by setting his critics a 'poser'; he was rather referring them to their ability to recognise the truth for themselves, if they would but honestly take the trouble to think it out.

Jesus' authority is the authority of people's own hearts and their deepest longings. Summing up his experience of life, Somerset Maughan said, 'I have gone a long way round to discover what everybody else knew already'. Christianity is in part knowing profoundly what people already know in their heart of hearts to be true: that love is better than hate, faith better than cynicism, hope better than despair, forgiveness nobler than spite, and sharing more satisfying than hoarding.

The longer the disciples were with Jesus, the more convinced they became of his rightful authority over their lives. Valuing human individuality, Jesus' authority did not mean regimentation. He did not seek to make James like John, or Thomas like Peter. Nor had his authority anything to do with authoritarianism. It is almost always those, like tyrants and dictators, who possess no real authority of character, who resort to authoritarian methods, who seek to impose patterns of behaviour and thought on other people. What Captain Scott said of Edward Wilson, 'He has by sheer force of character achieved a position of authority over the others, whilst retaining their warmest affections', was even truer of Jesus.

The only kind of authority which is likely to be taken seriously in a scientific, pragmatic age, is the kind Jesus indicated for his teaching. Jesus knew that worthwhile authority involves the free consent of people. 'Whoever has the will to do the will of God (as I am revealing it to you), shall know whether my teaching comes from Him or is merely my own.' [12] Those who were prepared to follow him, to accept him as the authoritative guide on matters of faith and conduct, discovered that he was not only the *Way*, but also the *Truth*. What he said and promised stood the test of experience. They also found *Life* enlarged and enriched.

The thoughtful child who asks, 'Why should or shouldn't I do this?' will not accept as an answer, 'Because I say so'. But if a sensible reason is offered, although the teenager may not agree or obey, he will at least inwardly respect such authority.

The truths that Jesus taught about life are valid, not simply because the Church or the Bible says so. They are valid because they speak to our condition and satisfy our deepest needs. The sayings of Jesus are not so much commandments as precise statements about the nature of life, admittedly often expressed pictorially. The statement that sand is a bad foundation and that rock is a good foundation which can be trusted, is neither dogma nor theory. It is a description of reality which those who are observant recognise as being true.

When all the unpleasant and depressing things that can be said about human nature have been said, the fact still remains that there is something in people that is capable of being

fascinated, lured and ultimately claimed by Jesus. It is significant
that even those who derided Jesus, and those who tried hard to
convince themselves that they were justified in having nothing
to do with him, still could not forget what he said. The theme of
a book entitled *Ideas have Legs,* was that if ideas are true, nothing
will ultimately stop them. They will pursue and haunt us. So it
was with the ideas Jesus let loose in the world. They were so
disconcertingly true.

'Love your enemies and pray for your persecutors.'[13] Though
costly, that is a saying that makes sense. In the strip cartoon,
Andy's stage boss kept slapping him across the chest whenever
they met. Finally Andy had had enough. He said to his friend
Amos, 'I am going to put a stick of dynamite in my vest pocket.
The next time he slaps me, he is going to get his hand blown
off!' So it is with the dynamite of hatred. It not only disrupts
private and community life, it finally consumes those who
harbour it. A far more common cause of heart disease than what
people eat, is what is eating them!

'Freely you have received, freely give.'[14] That makes sense
too. Jesus wanted people to turn privilege and plenty into an
opportunity for friendship and brotherliness through sharing
what they have. 'Social righteousness is really a matter of table
manners. We ought not to glut ourselves while others hunger.
Pass the bread please.'[15] 'He that loseth his life for my sake shall
find it.'[16] Personal experience confirms the wisdom of this
paradox. We find ourselves when we lose ourselves in purposes
larger than ourselves, purposes which enrich our common life.
We need to love as much as we need to be loved. Selfishness is
destructive of all that is lovely. It is a principle of death. The
selfish person is the shrinking person. If we are not concerned for
anything or anyone besides Number One, that number will be
reduced to an inconsequential zero.

'Always treat others as you would want them to treat you.'[17]
Within the context of the Christian faith, the Golden Rule can
be a noble guide. John Hunter, the distinguished eighteenth-

century Scottish doctor, used to say to his students, 'Never perform an operation on another person which under similar circumstances you would not have performed on yourself'. Home-life and industrial relationships would be greatly enriched if husbands would treat wives, or employers would treat employees, as they would want to be treated themselves if roles were reversed. In their saner moments most people, even those who are anti-god and anti-church, recognise the wisdom of Jesus' moral teaching. His way of life is not at all easy, but that does not alter our conviction that it is the best way.

I personally have found nothing in the teaching of Jesus which does not verify itself as true in my own experience. I have also discovered in experience no truth of major importance about life which is *not* to be found in the teaching of Jesus. When such a thing happens dozens of times, one comes to trust such a mind. Jesus has won for me, and many other people, the highest authority there is—the authority of insight tested and proved in practice.

Malcolm Muggeridge, who for many years, in his caustic and witty way, had railed against the churches and their 'superstitions', finally published a statement which astonished many who knew him. 'All I can say as one ageing and singularly unimportant fellow-man, is that I have conscientiously looked far and wide, inside and outside my own head and heart, and I have found nothing other than this man and his words which offers any answer to the dilemma of this tragic, troubled time. If his light has gone out, then as far as I am concerned, there is no light.'[18]

To those who press the query of Jesus' authority over their lives, I would say, 'If you know a finer authority which you are prepared to accept, then listen to him and lead us all to him. But if not, Jesus claims and deserves your loyalty and devotion'.

At that critical period in the life of Jesus when many of his followers left him because of the costs and risks involved, Jesus said to his twelve closest friends, 'Will you also go away?' It was then that Peter answered, 'Lord to whom shall we go? Your words are words of eternal life'.[19]

Notes and References

1   Matthew 8:5f
2   Luke 4:35
3   Luke 7:48
4   John 3:2
5   Matthew 7:28,29
6   John 2:25
7   John 7:16
8   Matthew 5:21,22
9   John 13:28
10 Matthew 7:24
11 Matthew 21:24
12 John 7:17
13 Matthew 5:44
14 Matthew 10:8 (K.J.)
15 George Buttrick
16 Matthew 10:39 (K.J.)
17 Matthew 7:12
18 *Jesus Rediscovered*
19 John 6:66-68

6

A Master Teacher

Policemen have offered many strange excuses to their superiors for their failure to arrest some offender, but surely few can compare with the extraordinary reason offered by the temple police. We could not arrest Jesus for 'no man ever spoke as this man speaks'.[1] Astonishing words from the lips of men who were accustomed, by the nature of their work, to pay as little heed to glib blarney as to swearing and cursing. The sheer moral force of what Jesus had said, had over-awed them. The depth yet simplicity of his teaching made a profound impression. 'Where does he get this wisdom from?'[2] they asked.

Since human language is inadequate to describe God as he actually is, those who speak of God face a dilemma. They can attempt to use precise metaphysical and theological language, which may be intelligible to professional theologians and philosophers, but certainly not to the man in the pew or the street. Or, like Jesus and the biblical writers, they can use metaphorical and pictorial language, the kind of language which, though not as precise, can make eternal truths come alive for ordinary folk.

A distinguished clergyman who was addressing simple Dalesmen in the Lake District is reported to have begun by reminding them one Sunday that they were surrounded by an 'apodeixis of theopratic omnipotence'. I am certain few of his hearers would learn much from that pompous introduction. When another divine of equal scholarship finished his sermon in a Scottish kirk, an old woman asked her friend, 'Well what did you think of that?' The reply was emphatic. 'I heard only the first two sentences and I thanked my Maker that I was too deaf to hear any more.' Had Jesus spoken about God as the 'Principle of Concretion', or the 'Ground of Being', or as being 'omniscient, omnipotent and omnipresent', or if he had talked about life and death in the remote academic language of the philosophical classroom, it is extremely doubtful if the common people would have heard him 'so gladly'. But instead he used numerous stories about everyday life to express the greatest of thoughts. He used key metaphors like 'Father' and 'Shepherd' to communicate profound truths about the Maker of heaven and earth.

Unwittingly most of us talk in metaphors every day of our lives. We speak of 'being in the same boat', of being 'green with envy', of a child or an adult being 'a pain in the neck'. Economists speak of 'frozen assets', 'floating the pound'; town-planners of 'bottle-necks' and 'concrete jungles'. Though none of these phrases is literally true, they do convey quickly and reasonably accurately, ideas which can be readily understood by ordinary folk. Jesus knew better than most how symbolism is the gateway to the human imagination: 'I am the bread of life . . . the light of the world'.

Because Jesus' interpretation of the Jewish scriptures contradicted at times that of the Jewish religious leaders, Jesus was finally forbidden to preach in the synagogues. He taught therefore mostly in the open air, at street corners and by the lakeside. Unlike present day ministers who are privileged to have an assembled congregation, open-air speakers have first to persuade people to stop and listen. Unless their teaching is arresting, they will never attract, let alone hold an audience. Dullness spells failure. As Robert Louis Stevenson said, 'What you cannot vivify, you should omit'.

Jesus had the ability to catch and hold the interest of people. He had mastered the art of beginning from where they were and of speaking in terms they could understand. Knowing how a good illustration lingers in the memory far longer than an abstract dissertation, Jesus embodied his message in everyday secular stories about kings, slaves, debtors, farmers, fisherfolk and housewives. Mark tells us, 'He never spoke to them except in parables'.[3]

In every generation there have been abstract condemnations of human greed and pride. Most have been forgotten, but not so the rich man who 'feasted sumptuously every day' while a poor man Lazarus, covered with sores, begged at his gate.[4] Nor has the other rich man who said to himself, 'You have ample goods laid up for many years. Take your ease. Eat, drink and be merry'.[5] Speaking to those who had what we would call a holier-than-thou' attitude, he told an unforgettable story about a Pharisee and a tax-gatherer who went up to the temple to pray.[6] When a lawyer asked 'Who is my neighbour?' he did not enter into an abstract discussion. He told instead about a man being mugged on a highway.[7] He let the story do the teaching. Shakespeare once tagged a salutary lesson to the end of one of his plays— Romeo and Juliet. He pointed out that the young people died because the old people quarrelled. But the play by itself makes that point very powerfully. When it is performed, the unnecessary moralising is usually omitted.

Jesus also used telling figures of speech to vivify the great truths he wanted to communicate, to highlight the human condition. Had he simply said, 'Charity should never be obtrusive', or 'Judge yourself before passing judgment on others', his words would probably have made little impact and been quickly forgotten. But the telling phrases he used jolted his hearers and became etched in their minds: 'When you do some act of charity, do not announce it with a flourish of trumpets'.[8] 'Why do you look at the speck of sawdust in your brother's eye with never a thought for the great plank in your own?'[9] The characters in Jesus' parables and the power of his imagery still grip and challenge our consciences.

The early years in the life of Jesus are often referred to as the 'Silent Years', for little is thought to be known of Jesus, up until about the age of thirty. But are these years not the most vocal? Are not many of his parables based on boyhood memories of his mother baking bread in the oven, and losing a coin one day? 'Consider the lilies,'[10] said Jesus. Where did he first see these flowers but on the slopes of the hills around Nazareth? Jesus also recalled the labourers standing in the village square waiting to be hired, the young children playing at weddings and, when they tired of that, playing at funerals; goats and sheep being separated; a sheep being lost and the shepherd going out in the wind and the rain to scour the hills for it. What rejoicing there was when he found it. Was it one of Jesus' boyhood friends who left home for some far country across the hills? Obviously still vivid in Jesus' memory was the lad's father trudging down the lane each night at sunset, day after day, month after month, hoping that his son might one day return home.

The skilled builder, said Jesus, does not build on a foundation of loose sand or without calculating the cost. Does the use of such figures of speech from the skilled trades confirm what tradition says about the silent years, that Jesus worked as a carpenter? (In those days a carpenter usually meant a builder of houses.)

An old woman said to Dr Thomas Guthrie, 'The parts of the Bible I like best, are the "likes"'. She spoke for thousands: 'The Kingdom of heaven is like a grain of mustard seed'[11]; 'like yeast'[12]; 'like treasure hid in a field'[13]; 'You are salt to the earth'.[14] These metaphors and striking phrases have become deeply embedded in our language. G. K. Chesterton scribbled in his private papers:

> There was a man who dwelt in the East centuries ago,
> And now I cannot look at a sheep or a sparrow,
> A lily or a cornfield, a raven or a sunset,
> A vineyard or a mountain, without thinking of Him.

We still talk about good Samaritans, about passing by on the other side, about bearing the burden and heat of the day. Some use their 'talents' rightly; others hide them 'under a bushel', or leave things to 'the eleventh hour'. These everyday phrases are straight out of the teaching of Jesus. He appealed to the intelligence through the imagination. Wild lilies, birds nesting, seed growing, candles, figs, thistles—these were the texts of the greatest teacher and preacher this world has known. Thus he sought to show his contemporaries 'the treasure hid in the field' of everyday life.

Jesus' aim in his teaching was to awaken people to simple truths, long familiar but neglected, distrusted or denied. He selected and rephrased in matchless metaphors and images, truths taught centuries before by the Psalmist and the Jewish prophets:

> that caring love is at the heart of all things;
> that though we pass through the valley of the shadow, we need fear no evil;
> that God is our refuge and strength, a present help in time of trouble.

He knew that the number of new things we need to learn is often less important than the many old things of which we need to be reminded.

As it was once expressed rather crudely, but penetratingly, 'He scratched where people itched'. He spoke in a simple way about the deepest things in life, about faith, hope, love, justice, joy and peace. He shed light on the questions people were asking. His message was infused with life and death interest.

Many of his parables were told in an atmosphere of intense controversy. At times he would force his listeners to reformulate the question. More important, he said, than 'Who is my neighbour?' is the question 'What does it mean to be a neighbour?' At other times, such was his skill as a teacher that he would hide the person or persons he was addressing in the story in such a way that, in passing judgment on the characters in the parable, they unwittingly passed judgment on themselves.[15]

It was said of a speaker whose mode of life belied his words, 'Nothing sounds so dreadful as the right phrase on the wrong lips'. That could not be said of Jesus. His example was even more compelling than his method or message. What he said had the full backing of his life. Many to whom he talked about prayer could recall seeing him going off early in the morning to be alone with God in the hills. Many to whom he spoke about faith in God knew how quietly and fearlessly he walked amid all the plotting of his enemies. Many to whom he talked about forgiveness knew how gently he had dealt with Mary Magdalene. His life was as unforgettable as his words.

Notes and References

1   John 7.46
2   Matthew 13:54
3   Mark 4:34
4   Luke 16:19-31
5   Luke 12:19
6   Luke 18:10f
7   Luke 10:29f
8   Matthew 6:2
9   Matthew 7:4
10 Matthew 6:28
11 Matthew 13:31
12 Matthew 13:33
13 Matthew 13:44
14 Matthew 5:13
15 Luke 15:1

A Man's Man

Right from the word go, Pilate wanted to have nothing to do with the trial of Jesus. He told the Jews to try him themselves, but they refused for they could not authorise death by crucifixion. Next he sent Jesus to Herod, hoping Herod might try him. But Herod did not oblige either. He immediately returned Jesus.

Pilate's concern for Jesus was not casual. Jesus attracted and disturbed him. Far from idly washing his hands of the case, he tried every possible means to save Jesus from capital punishment. He reminded the Jews of their privilege at Passover to have a condemned person released, one of their own choice. He suggested Jesus. But they clamoured for Barabbas, a bandit.

Having spoken with Jesus again, Pilate went out and courageously informed the assembled throng that he found no fault in Jesus. But the Jews would not accept this. 'He claimed to be a king,'[1] they said. Then they protested their loyalty to Caesar! One can imagine the cynical look on Pilate's face as he heard that. He had cause to know only too well the embittered hostility of the majority of Jews to the overlordship of Rome. They had stubbornly refused to allow images of the Roman Emperor to be erected in the Holy City. They were most reluctant to pay taxes to Rome. But now in order to get rid of Jesus, the Jews cry, 'We have no king but Caesar!'[2] Pilate must have thought, 'What pious hypocrites'.

Pilate then ordered Jesus to be scourged. He perhaps thought such brutal torture might be acceptable to the Jews as an alternative to the death sentence. Bringing Jesus, bruised and bleeding out onto the porch, Pilate said, 'Behold the Man'.[3] Gaze on him. Can you really see this battered figure, this broken man as your king? But it was not enough. They still demanded his crucifixion.

Not only in his account of the trial of Jesus, but right through his Gospel, John keeps stressing that Jesus was a real man, that he knew what it was to suffer, to be discouraged and frustrated. Though well aware of depths in Jesus which transcend human understanding, yet John constantly reminds his readers that Jesus was subject to the normal temptations and limitations of mankind.

He was limited in knowledge and knew it. In a saying which is assuredly authentic, he declares himself ignorant of the day and the hour of the end of the world. There is no indication either that he transcended the knowledge of the natural world common to his Palestinian contemporaries.

Jesus grew from infancy to manhood like any other person. He had to learn language as any other child does. Like all Jewish children, it was on the Old Testament scriptures that his soul was nourished and in its thought-forms that he expressed his faith in God. When he had problems he had to think them through like the rest of us. He enjoyed the company of friends. When one of them died, he wept unashamedly. When temptations came, he retired into a quiet place and prayed that God's will might be done. It is significant that in the temptations to which Jesus was subject at the beginning of his ministry, the tempter is depicted as appealing to such human weaknesses as bodily appetite, ambition and spiritual pride.[4] 'He was in all points tempted like as we are.'[5] He was fully human. This needs to be stressed, for at various times in the Church's history, the Church's opinion of human beings has fallen so low that theologians divorced Jesus, not only from physical hunger, weariness and death, but from the normal processes of human growth. One group of Christians in the early Church, the Docetics, believed Jesus' mind, will and spirit were divine, but that his body was not a real human body. They said that when he walked he left no footprints and that on Calvary he only seemed to die. Not so, say the Gospel records.

The record of the last journey to Jerusalem and on to Calvary is almost unbearable to read because so intensely human. There was no fake in Jesus' tears, no make-belief about the agonising decision he had to make in Gethsemane. He left it to us to romanticise the agony of that hour, to sing 'Sweet hour of prayer'! There was no pretence about his stumbling with the Cross. His wounds bled profusely as those of any other person. The excruciating pain, the awful thirst, were all too real. Pangs of thirst are among the most terrible we can know. With hunger there comes a faintness, a numbing of the vital powers, but thirst will not allow one moment of insensibility.

'I thirst.'[6] This cry from the Cross has occasionally been interpreted metaphorically. Ancient prayers speak of Jesus on Calvary 'thirsting for our salvation', but is not this to read more into these words than John intended? When on the Cross he became thirsty, it was real thirst. When nails were driven through his hands they hurt, and real blood flowed from his wounds. When the soldiers dropped the Cross with a sickening thud into the hole prepared for it, how Jesus must have winced. It is not simply mistaken piety that casts doubts on the full humanity of Jesus, it is heresy, and has been so labelled by the Church since the Council of Chalcedon in AD 451.

An eminent Britisher once described Jesus as 'a king on a ruddy donkey'. The rather crude description simply heightens the fact that there is nothing in history quite like the strange union of humility and majesty, humanity and divinity that we see in Jesus. Born not in a palace, but in a squalid stable with cattle looking on, he appeared no different from a hundred million other babies. A lowly birth but what a stir it caused in heaven. The heir to 'many mansions', he was brought up with six other children in a one-roomed house, the kind Jesus described in one of his parables as 'small enough to be lit by a single lamp'.[7] (One of his brothers, James, is thought by many to be the author of the Epistle of James). The name Jesus, to which he answered as a child and as a man, and under which he was crucified, was a common one. Some scholars believe Barabbas' Christian name was also Jesus. (Barrabas means 'son of Abbas'.) Jesus, a name shared by many of his contemporaries, yet now a name which is above every name.[8]

Some of the words the Church has coined at various times to describe the uniqueness and supremacy of Jesus, words like 'prophet, priest and king', are almost unintelligible to ordinary folk today. They have lost much of their original significance. When separated from the very human words Jesus used to talk about himself—servant, brother, worker—they can in fact be misleading. It is perhaps because words like servant and worker highlight the humanity of Jesus rather than his uniqueness, that the Church has seldom developed their use.

Turgenev told how once in a vision there stood beside him a man he was sure was Jesus. But he had 'a face like all men's faces . . . . What sort of a Christ is this?' he thought. 'Such an ordinary, ordinary man . . . . But then I realised that just such a face, a face like all men's faces, is the face of Christ.' And yet, since the human face mirrors character, there must have been an amazing graciousness and strength about Jesus' face.

He was so like us and yet so different. He lived in our world but carried with him the aura of another. In the Gospels it is not his self-consciousness that strikes us, but his deep and continual consciousness of God. Worn out he fell asleep in the stern of a fishing boat. So very human, and yet a few minutes later in a violent storm, he is complete master of the situation. Introducing a certain incident in the life of Jesus, John tells how Jesus knew 'that the Father had entrusted everything to him, and that he had come from God and was going back to God. . . . '[9] This is a truly cosmic introduction. What heights we climb! Just as we reach the peak, expecting to follow the story of the Transfiguration, or the raising of Jairus' daughter, we pass into what many would regard as the sheerest commonplace. 'He took a towel and girded himself and washed the disciples' feet.'[10] The strange blend of lowliness and grandeur in Jesus was gloriously unique.

Jesus stressed that he had come not to be served but to serve; that he was meek and lowly of heart. Yet he also arrogated to himself a position transcending all the wisdom of the centuries. 'My task is to bear witness to the truth.'[11] 'I am the way, the truth and the life.'[12] 'Heaven and earth will pass away; my words will never pass away.'[13] The centuries have proved him right. His teaching was never more relevant than it is today. Though the world has changed in incalculable ways, it has not outgrown him or his words. The proud theories of the science of one generation may be the jest of the next generation. But not so the teachings of Jesus. They have stood the severest of all tests, the test of time. What Jesus taught about God and life in Nazareth and Jerusalem is still relevant in Dornoch and Edinburgh. What he taught about faith, hope and love on the banks of the Jordan is still relevant on the banks of the Clyde.

Studdert Kennedy wrote, 'If a man or woman, or an age of men and women, reject the character of Christ, they do it at their own peril and time makes the peril plain. An age of luxury may reject his discipline, but time makes clear that they are wrong. An age of materialism may reject his idealism, but their children will come seeking it again. An age of puritanism may condemn his gaiety and gentleness, but the pendulum will swing back again. An age of scientific knowledge may spurn his simplicity, but men will come back with outstretched arms and empty hearts to ask the real questions that learning leaves unanswered for the soul. If a man or woman rejects the Character, I find myself wondering what is the matter with them. . . . They may reject orthodox theology because it puts their minds in a muddle, and does not seem worthy of Jesus . . . but if they turn from him however as Man, man with a capital M, Man as he ought to be, then I wonder about them, what's wrong?'[14]

When a precious stone in the rough is taken from the dark where it often seems dull and dingy, into the light where the sunshine can break through it, a splendour and beauty never imagined before are suddenly revealed. Likewise in Jesus, human nature was carried out of the dark into the light, and people glimpsed what a wonderful thing it can become when infused with the Spirit of God, when love of neighbour goes hand in hand with love of self, when giving comes before getting, when concern for the wrong-doer is greater than concern for one's own injury. Here was a man who was completely obedient to God and totally committed to his fellow-men and women. Becoming fully human is becoming what Jesus was. In Jesus we have God's ultimate word about who we are, and about how we ought to live.

The god-like in Jesus, the transcendent dimension to his life, will continue to fascinate the centuries. But so too will his humanity. Shakespeare's words could well be used to describe Jesus[15]:

> His life was gentle, and the elements
> So mix'd in him that Nature might stand up
> And say to all the world,
>   'This was a man'.

Notes and References

1   John 19:12
2   John 19:15
3   John 19:5
4   Luke 4:1-12
5   Hebrews 4:15 (K.J.)
6   John 19:29
7   Luke 15:8
8   Philippians 2:9
9   John 13:3
10   John 13:4
11   John 18:37
12   John 14:6
13   Matthew 24:35
14   *Food for the Fed-Up*, p. 77-78
15   *Julius Caesar* v:iii:71

8

A Heretic

A photograph is a likeness. So is a portrait. But how differently each may present the subject. The one is a single pose, caught by the camera. In the other we have the same subject, observed not through a mere lens, but caught in the mind and eye of the artist. A portrait reveals the character of the subject as the artist sees it. He composes his picture by selecting and concentrating on those characteristics which he regards as most typical.

The Gospels are such portraits, carefully composed pictures of the life of Jesus. John says, 'There were indeed many other signs that Jesus performed in the presence of his disciples, which are not recorded in this book. Those here written have been recorded in order that you may hold the faith that Jesus is the Christ, the Son of God, and that through this faith you may possess life by his name'.[1] Here speaks the selective artist. John makes it clear why he included in his record certain events and conversations.

The Gospels have been aptly called 'The Second Book of Genesis', for they tell of the time when a new creation came into being, of how God spoke a second time, 'Let there be light'. How bright was the light God lit at Bethlehem! Those who wrote the Gospels, and others who had been 'walking in darkness', had come to see in Jesus the glory of God. The longer they were with him, the more persuaded they became that they were in the presence of one who was nearer to God than anyone they had ever met, one who had the love of God in his hands and the wisdom of God on his lips.

Before meeting Jesus, they would have regarded it as blasphemy for any ordinary Jew to set himself at the focal point of mankind's long search for truth and God. They would have deemed it sheer presumption for any carpenter to announce that with his ministry the reign of God had arrived, or that with his appearance the great promises of their scriptures were coming true.

There are those who maintain that Jesus never in fact made such claims, that they were all later attributed to him by his admiring followers, in order to communicate what they themselves had come to believe about Jesus. Now the Gospels are certainly intensely personal memoirs. Matthew, Mark and Luke, in writing their account of the Life of Jesus, reflect the Jewish style of reporting, a style concerned to preserve as nearly as possible in their original form the actual words of their nation's 'wise men'. It was the custom of Jewish teachers to encourage their disciples to memorise their teaching.

In John's Gospel, history and interpretation are inextricably interwoven. Starting from such utterances of Jesus as 'I am the bread of life . . .',[2] and 'I am the light of the world . . .',[3] John, half a century after the resurrection, proceeds to give his contemporaries a systematic summary of Christian teaching as he himself, under the inspiration of the Risen Christ, conceived it. In this way John interprets for his contemporaries the cosmic mind of Jesus. This explains why the speeches of Jesus in John's Gospel sound different from those in the other three Gospels.

Had Jesus not claimed that he was uniquely related to God, had he not spoken with more than human authority, Matthew, Mark and Luke would never have concocted such claims. Nor would such a devout Jew as John ever have composed his inspired airs concerning the divinity of Jesus, if the original themes had not been an essential part of the teaching of Jesus.

Some in our day would like to dispense with all talk of the divinity of Jesus. They would have us return to the 'simplicities of Galilee' and the ethics of the Sermon on the Mount. The American President Thomas Jefferson had a very high regard for Jesus whom he called 'the most sublime personality of whom history has a record'. In a book which he published under the title, *The Life and Morals of Jesus of Nazareth,* he carefully selected

certain passages from the four Gospels. He did this in such a way
that his 'Jefferson Bible' deleted every reference to Jesus as more
than teacher. But such a merely human Christ is a made-up
figure, a piece of artificial selection. We can no more eliminate
from the Gospel records the references to Jesus' uniqueness and
divinity than we can remove the watermark from a pound note.
The Gospels make it abundantly clear that what most fascinated
people, was not in fact Jesus' high ethical standards and teaching, but the growing certainty that in Jesus something was
expressed in and through a human life, which was yet other than
humanity. It was in God's name that he addressed his words of
promise to his hearers and urged on them his compelling
demands. Time and time again he spoke consciously and deliberately with divine authority. The parable which he told about
God sending messengers to the vineyard, speaks a language that
transcends history.[4] One by one the messengers (the prophets)
were shamefully treated, until at last God sent his own son, the
clear inference of the parable being that he was this well-beloved
son.

Time and time again he claimed for himself what Jews
believed was the prerogative of God alone, the right to forgive
sins.[5] He dared to criticise temple practices, which for the
orthodox Jew was like criticising God himself. He not only
dispensed with many of the regulations governing the Sabbath,
like fasting and ritual cleansing, but he adopted towards the Law
of Moses an authoritatively critical attitude that no rabbi would
ever have done. Every Jew was as much subject to the Mosaic
Law as to God. The tension between Jesus and the Jewish leaders
was heightened by the fact that the Pharisees were at that time
very much on the defensive. They were determined to preserve
the Law and the way of life it generated, in the midst of a
surrounding sea of heathenism. In some countries Jews were
attempting to form an alliance between the Jewish Law and
Greek philosophy, attempting to prove that Greek philosophy
was itself derived from the books of Moses. In the homeland of

the faith such liberalism was regarded as the first step on the road to infidelity.

When the guardians of the Jewish tradition in the Holy City heard that Jesus was claiming the right to revise and give free interpretation to the Mosaic Law, 'You have learned that our forefathers were told . . . but what I tell you is this',[6] they not surprisingly regarded him as an infidel. To understand something of the shock which such words must originally have caused, imagine a young minister rising in the General Assembly of the Church of Scotland and saying, 'The Bible says . . . but I say'. The claim that Jesus stood in a unique relationship with God, characterises not just a few of his sayings, but the whole manner of his conversation. 'When that day comes many will say to me, "Lord, Lord, did we not prophesy in your name?"'[7] Here Jesus pictures himself as the final judge. That Caiaphas and his close associates should have regarded Jesus as a heretic and a blasphemer, is surely proof that he did make staggering claims for himself. The things Jesus did, like cleansing the temple and breaking the Sabbath, upset the Jewish hierarchy, but so too did the outrageous things he said on these occasions. 'It was works of this kind done on the Sabbath that stirred the Jews to persecute Jesus . . . he was not only breaking the Sabbath, but, by calling God his own Father, he claimed equality with God.'[8] He even dared to use the familiar word 'Abba',[9] the equivalent of our modern 'Daddy'. To speak of God in such an intimate way was in the eyes of the Jewish leaders sheer blasphemy. So great was the gulf in first century Judaism between God in his holiness and man in his sinfulness, that ordinary worshippers did not even dare to use the word 'God'. They said, 'O Most High'.

During the rigged trial of Jesus, held in a secret place, in the grim small hours before daybreak, Caiaphas, surrounded by his close associates, put to the accused the question, 'Are you the Messiah?' At first Jesus declined to reply. 'If I tell you,' he finally said, 'You will not believe me.'[10] Perceiving that their minds were closed and their hearts hardened, Jesus felt that nothing was to be gained from further debate. Jesus had had his say, and he had said it most gloriously. But his judgment now told him that in the face of such a hostile prejudiced court, further words would be of little or no avail.

Caiaphas' intense dislike of Jesus is further indication of how great were the differences between the religion of Caiaphas and the religion of Jesus. The former was for the most part locked up in a building, in formal ritual and a complicated code of rules. The religion of Jesus, on the other hand, was out in the open air where people lived and worked. It was a loosely-knit, informal fellowship of people willing to follow in his way—the way of caring and sharing, giving and forgiving, work and worship, loving God with all their hearts, minds and souls, and their neighbours as themselves.

Jesus' thinking and way of life were so much at cross-purposes with that of the Jewish hierarchy, that they finally decided to get rid of him. He was not only undermining the very foundations of their faith, he was a threat to their national integrity. The time for letting him suffer the consequence of his arrogance had come. The kingdom of justice and brotherhood which he hoped to establish, a brotherhood which included Gentiles and Samaritans, was culturally unacceptable and religiously blasphemous.

Notes and References

1   John 20:30-31
2   John 6:48
3   John 8:12
4   Luke 20:9f
5   Matthew 9:2
6   Matthew 5:21
7   Matthew 7:22
8   John 5:18
9   Mark 14:36
10 Luke 22:67

9

A Glutton and Drinker

Bunuel's film 'The Milky Way' was described as anti-Christian and anti-religious. At one stage there is a cut-back to New Testament times. An open-air lunch is in progress. Jesus is the life and soul of the gathering. When the guests call on him to make a speech, he rises amid cheers and, with a twinkle in his eye, tells what some scholars now believe was a funny story—the parable of the unjust steward. The audience doubles with laughter.

Some viewers objected to Bunuel's portrait of a vibrant Christ sparkling with wit. They felt it bore little relation to the Christ of the Gospels. But are the portraits so very different? Think of the humour of many of Jesus' word pictures: ungainly camels trying to go through the eye of a needle; people with great logs in their eyes trying to remove specks from other people's eyes; the religious leaders straining at little gnats and swallowing camels; blind people attempting to lead other blind people. Recall also his telling of a man who lit a candle and then went and put it under a bushel. If we modernise that, by imagining him switching on the light, and then in order to save electricity wrapping the light shade in black paper, we will more readily glimpse the humour.

The sadness of the last tragic days in the life of Jesus, the kneeling in agony in Gethsemane, the jeering crowds in Pilate's court, the excruciating pain of crucifixion, has unfortunately left the impression that Jesus was predominantly a 'Man of sorrows acquainted with grief', and that it is somehow irreverent to think of him as enjoying a good meal and a joke. But how different is the portrait in the earlier chapters of the New Testament. There we catch glimpses of a man of smiles acquainted with laughter.

Jesus' joy was as striking as his compassion. *Tharsete,* meaning 'cheer up', was his watchword. He criticised the Pharisees for their glum faces, as though in mourning for their faith. Jesus was such a happy, colourful personality, so much in love with life, that people wanted him with them, not only in times of sickness and bereavement, but also as a guest at wedding banquets. Had he been dull and humourless—a lean ascetic with a sad look, one who despised the good things of this world—he would not have been invited. Little children, publicans and sinners would also have found ways of avoiding him. The fact that he and his followers enjoyed festivities and parties scandalised the religious people of his day.

Jesus did not fit the contemporary picture of preacher or prophet. He was too cheerful to be a holy man. 'John's disciples are much given to fasting and the practice of prayer . . . but yours eat and drink.'[1] Jesus taught and exercised temperance with regard to food and drink, but there is no denying that he did taste these gifts with joy: 'The old wine is good'.[2] Because by Pharisaic standards he seemed to take excessive delight in eating and drinking, they called him 'a glutton and a drinker'.[3] If, as some scholars believe, Jesus had a direct connection in his early years with an Essene-like movement of the separatist type represented at Qumran, he certainly was not unduly influenced by it. Jesus was no separatist. Nor did he display any of the normal traits of the ascetic. Whereas John the Baptist and the Essenes called on people to lead an austere life, Jesus' concern was to enrich it with colour, compassion and meaning. When asked to describe himself, he chose the term 'bride-groom'.[4] Eyes brightened and hearts rejoiced at his coming. He left a trail of gladness wherever he went. When the Pharisees criticised him for the company he kept—'This fellow welcomes sinners and eats with them'[5]—Jesus told them of the wonderful meal arranged to celebrate the prodigal's return. The fatted calf was killed, music and dancing followed.[6]

Jesus seems to have been very conscious of man's inability or unwillingness to enter into 'the joy of the Lord'. Several of his parables deal with people refusing to come to the party or being disqualified from entering the wedding feast. The foolish virgins missed the party because life had dried up, they had no oil in their lamps.[7] The man without wedding garments missed the party because he lacked the courtesy to accept and wear the appropriate clothing which was freely offered.[8] The elder brother missed the music and the feasting because he was 'angry and refused to go in'.[9]

In his farewell discourse to his disciples, Jesus said, 'I have spoken thus to you, so that my joy may be in you and that your joy may be complete'.[10] Christianity began as a religion of joy. The Greek noun *chara,* meaning 'joy', appears more than fifty times in the New Testament; *charein,* meaning 'to rejoice', appears over seventy times. What a tragedy that twenty centuries later, the term 'happy Christian' should, in certain communities, have a hollow ring; that Christianity should be equated with restrictions rather than acts of caring love, with congealed solemnity rather than smiling faces, with boring tedium rather than a joyous *Te Deum.*

> All people that on earth do dwell
> Sing to the Lord with *cheerful* voice
> Him serve with *mirth,* his praise forth tell
> Come ye before him and *rejoice.*

A worshipper tells of sitting behind a small boy who, during the opening hymn, was turning round, smiling. He was not kicking the pew in front, nor was he tearing the hymnbook apart, nor was he rummaging through his mother's handbag. He was just smiling. Finally his mother jerked him round. Smacking him on the hand, she said, 'Stop that grinning. You are in church!' As the tears rolled down his cheeks she added, 'That is better', and returned to her prayers.

Christians not only misrepresent Christ when they refuse to care and forgive, they also misrepresent him when they spread unhappiness rather than radiate happiness, when they worship with solemnity akin to mourners. The quite un-Christian idea that God is displeased when people smile or enjoy themselves, that religion is incompatible with fun and laughter, has burdened the world with many unattractive saints. How apt was the comment of the little girl brought up in a very strict home: 'If I am extra good in heaven may I have some little devils in for tea now and then?'

Jesus, whom Peter called the prince of life, whom Paul called the pioneer of life, never thought of goodness as repression, or of religion as confining. Jesus conceived life as the eager running-out of the heart to love and laughter, to all that is good and generous, helpful and healing. 'I am come,' he said, 'that you might have life and have it more abundantly' [12]—not moribundantly.

Notes and References

 1   Luke 5:35
 2   Luke 5:39
 3   Luke 7:34
 4   Luke 5:34
 5   Luke 15:2
 6   Luke 15:26
 7   Matthew 25:1f
 8   Matthew 22:11f
 9   Luke 15:28
10   John 15:11
11   Psalm 100 (metrical version)
12   John 10:10

10

A Good Man

The genuinely good man! Is he not the most attractive of all? A domineering person is exhausting. Comics are good fun for a time. Then they pall. Cleverness has its place, but mere cleverness irritates. True goodness is, however, permanently satisfying, the wine of life.

In orthodox Jewish society a 'righteous man' was forbidden to have anything to do with the unrighteous. There was a sharp line of separation between the so-called saints and sinners, the 'goodies' and 'baddies'. The name Pharisee was derived from the Hebrew word 'parushim' meaning 'the separated ones'. Only the 'goodies' were welcome at synagogue worship. By birth and upbringing Jesus belonged to the righteous part of the community. With his family he was a regular worshipper in the synagogue. Jesus was well aware of the falsity of this division, which was accepted by his contemporaries, and of how readily it made for hypocrisy. It was so easy to be respectably righteous and yet at some essential points utterly godless. When the rich young ruler, who seems to have been imprisoned in his own self-righteousness, addressed Jesus as 'Good Master', Jesus said 'Why do you call me good? No one is good except God alone'.[1] A gentle rebuke, but profoundly significant.

Though Jesus was reluctant to be classified with society's 'goodies', there is no denying that he was a marvellously good and kind person. Ericsson, a close friend of Paganini, was a skilful violin-maker, but he had no ear for music. He once mended Paganini's violin, doing the job so well that it was almost better than before. When Paganini collected the violin, he started to play it. Workmen crowded the shop, spellbound. Even Ericsson cried at last, 'Paganini, I've an ear for music after all, for *that* kind of music'. So it was with Jesus. Even the 'baddies' in Palestine—the publicans and sinners—had an ear for life as Jesus lived it. They were attracted by the warmth, sincerity and spontaneity of his goodness. In the early Church the title *Christos,* meaning 'the Anointed One', or 'the Messiah', was sometimes misspelled as *Chrestos*—a happy mistake, for the Greek word chrestos means 'kind'. 'He went about doing good'[2]: that was how Peter summarised Jesus' life. Years later, in one of his letters, he highlighted certain aspects of Jesus' goodness.

Jesus 'left you an example; it is for you to follow in his steps. He committed no sin, he was convicted of no falsehood; when he was abused he did not retort with abuse; when he suffered he uttered no threats'.[3] The hands that had touched fevered heads, they pierced with nails; the heart which had never stopped loving, they broke on a tree; the eyes that wept over people's sorrows, they spat upon. Yet still he reviled not, he threatened not. Peter could not get over the wonder of it. Centuries later Dostoevsky shared his point of view: 'My creed is very simple. I believe there is nothing more beautiful, more profound, more sympathetic, more reasonable, more manly and more perfect than Christ'.

It is significant that the records we have of the life of Jesus tell us nothing of what Jesus looked like. They do not reveal how tall he was, whether he was well-built or slim, bearded or clean-shaven. But time and again we are told he loved and cared, gave and forgave. He healed the sick and comforted the bereaved. He had a profound concern for those burdened and toil-worn folk who reminded him of weary heavy-laden camels, of tired oxen dragging the plough day after day through stiff clay: 'Come to me all whose work is hard, whose load is heavy, and I will give you relief. Bend your necks to my yoke and learn of me'.[4] The evidence is strong that when Jesus met lepers or cripples, he so put himself in their place, that he really felt what it was like never again to see one's loved ones, never again to move freely about.

Most people have sympathy for those they know and like. The astonishing thing about Jesus was that he extended such compassion to his enemies. In all probability Jesus was not the first man the Roman centurion had crucified. The centurion would be accustomed to prisoners shrieking in agony, hurling their oaths and curses at the indifferent guards. But with this Galilean it was different. He had bravely endured the scourging and the driving-in of the cruel nails. The military virtues which the centurion had been taught to admire—courage, endurance, discipline and self-sacrifice—were all exhibited by Jesus. But these military virtues were transfigured into something sublime and unforgettable by the man's sheer goodness and his genuine concern for those who were doing this awful thing to him. 'Father forgive them; they do not know what they are doing.' [5] Though racked with pain, his loving spirit was still in control. The centurion realised that he would probably never see his like again. 'Beyond all doubt this man was innocent.' [6]

In *Oliver Twist*, Charley Bates, the jocular young rogue, and Bill Sikes, the hardened ruffian, both belonged to Fagan's gang of thieves. But after Nancy had been foully done to death by Bill Sikes, Charley Bates shuddered at his proffered handshake. 'Don't come near me,' said the boy, looking with horror at the murderer's face. His reaction was similar to one of the thieves who was crucified with Jesus. Jesus' ineffably tender prayer of forgiveness struck deep into his soul as nothing else had done in years. Here obviously was a good man. When his colleague in crime started cursing Jesus, he recoiled. Such callousness was more than he could stand. 'Look here,' he said, 'for us this is plain justice; we are paying the price of our misdeeds; but this man has done nothing wrong.' Then turning to Jesus he said, 'Remember me when you come to your throne'. [7] The impression Jesus had made throughout his life, held to the end. This dying thief turned to him as to one who could still help. Though nailed to a cross there was still something regal about Jesus.

The Roman procurator and his wife were also greatly impressed. Pilate said to the Jews, 'I find no fault in this man'.[8] Pilate's wife was also convinced of his innocence: 'Have nothing to do with that innocent man; I was much troubled on his account in my dreams last night'.[9] To condemn a person to death was for Pilate a mere act of administrative routine. Crucifixions in Palestine were frequent occurrences. Crosses were often seen dotted along roadsides. Yet there was a poise, a dignity, and an integrity about this man that was different. Pilate went to considerable lengths to try to release Jesus, but finally, to prevent an uprising, he agreed to his crucifixion.

When we meet someone who does not think forever of himself, who genuinely cares for others, who does not cry for vengeance, who is not greedy, lustful or prejudiced, it is superficial to assume that he does not experience the temptations which drag others down. Was it to refute such a mistaken idea that the writer to the Hebrews stressed how Jesus was tempted but without sin, how he was tested, but passed through the test? Robert Burns' love life was far from exemplary. Time and time again he succumbed to temptation. In this respect at least, Samuel Johnson led an exemplary life. It would, however, be mistaken to conclude that Johnson was never thus tempted. There is evidence to the contrary. To be tempted is an inevitable aspect of the human situation. Sin begins when our minds linger on wrong suggestions and derive pleasure from them. Paradoxically, the severity of temptation is felt, not by those who readily give in to it, but by those who resist it.

Jesus knew that if he spoke and lived as God wanted, he would become a target for all the resistance and antagonism of selfish people. Far from wanting to be the victim of such misunderstanding and abuse, Jesus was tempted at the beginning of his ministry to avoid conflict and suffering by becoming the kind of popular Messiah people wanted—a Superstar![10] The pictorial account of his temptations in the wilderness (which probably formed part of a private discourse with his intimate disciples), shows with what clarity of vision and strength of purpose Jesus set aside all conceptions of duty which were merely selfish, nationalistic or worldly. 'If you are God's Messiah provide some proof of it. You are hungry, and a great many people in this world are hungry. Why not a little bread perhaps, from these stones? You can do it. If you do, they will make you a king. Or what about some other spectacular sign? Show the worshippers in the temple precincts you are who you think you are, and who they hope you are; leap from this pinnacle, and appear among them, heaven-sent and unhurt! They want to see that sort of thing, and well you know it. You won't even bruise your foot. God will see to that. No cross that way, only a crown.' But Jesus did not yield to such devilish suggestions.

It is in such decisive moments that a person's faith is most clearly revealed. Gethsemane, when everything, including life itself, was at stake, was another occasion. 'My Father, if it is possible, let this cup [of suffering] pass me by.'[11] Perhaps to some extent it was fear of excruciating pain that prompted this cry. But was it not even more a fear of failure?

The Gospels may well be read as a series of incidents in which Jesus sought to align his will to the will of God. More than a hundred verses in John's Gospel are in the context of Jesus' profound love for his Father, and his complete dedication to his heavenly Father's purposes: 'My aim is not my own will, but the will of him who sent me'.[12] In the temple as a boy he sought to find out what God wanted him to do with his life. At his baptism he offered himself that God's purposes might be fulfilled. In the desert he sought to clarify his thoughts concerning the kind of Messiah God wanted him to be. In the last days of his life he fought a fierce battle with the human horror of a cruel and early death. A young man in love with life, he did not want to die. He had no martyr complex. In Gethsemane he was tempted to compromise a little, but at most he wavered for a moment. He knew that to turn back now would mean denying all he had stood for. He went on to pray, 'Not as I will, but as thou wilt'.[13]

His life began, continued and ended in obedience to the will of God. The assertion of Jesus' sinlessness is a negative way of expressing the reality of Jesus' dedication to God, for sin is essentially life in contradiction to how God would have us live.

Within people there are certain assurances and assumptions which are more nearly their real self than anything else—assurances about what is to be trusted, assumptions upon which life is constantly lived. These assurances and assumptions are not always identical with what they profess to believe. Their creed may be better or worse than their life. In the case of hypocrites, profession and practice are poles apart. When people's words and actions are consistent with these assurances and assumptions, then they are 'in-divid-uals' (not divided persons), either scoundrels or saints. Jesus was the true individual. With his life as well as his lips he prayed, 'Father thy will be done'.

When the Roman centurion said, 'This man is innocent'; when the dying thief said, 'This man has done nothing wrong'; when Pilate and his wife admitted that they could find no fault in Jesus—they had stumbled upon a truth, the full implications of which they did not however realise, that in the life of Jesus we have God's ultimate word about who man is and how he should live his life. Despite the pressures which Jesus' contemporaries, including the disciples, exerted on him, and despite the under-privileged and trying conditions in which he lived, Jesus never wavered from the way of caring love. He perfectly exemplified the love of God.

Notes and References

1　Luke 18:19
2　Acts 10:38
3　1 Peter 2:21f
4　Matthew 11:28
5　Luke 23:34
6　Luke 23:47

7   Luke 23:42
8   Luke 23:4 (K.J.)
9   Matthew 27:19
10   Matthew 4:1f
11   Matthew 26:39
12   John 5:30
13   Matthew 26:39

11

The Outcast

The taunting question which the Jewish leaders put to Jesus, 'Are we not right in saying that you are a Samaritan?'[1], would never have been asked had Jesus not time and time again sided with the Samaritans, a group of people with whom the Jews had no dealings. Their quarrel with the Samaritans had lasted seven hundred years. After Samaria fell to the Assyrians in 721 BC, the inhabitants of that city inter-married with the Assyrian settlers, thus mixing pure Jewish with foreign blood. For orthodox Jews with their exclusive marriage laws, this was so unforgiveable that they bitterly disowned the Samaritans. They tried to avoid all social contact with them. When they did meet, they treated them with every mark of contempt. Two hundred years later the Samaritans offered help in rebuilding the temple at Jerusalem. But the Jewish leaders of the returned exiles, snubbed them by turning them down flat. The Samaritans then responded in kind. They used so much political pressure that they got the rebuilding of the temple delayed for almost two decades.[2]

In the time of Jesus, 'Samaritan' was certainly not a word that the Jews coupled with 'good'. Though they lived next door to the Samaritans, they never thought of them as being neighbours. Their hostile feelings towards the Samaritans were summed up in the Jewish prayer, 'May I never set eyes on a Samaritan. May I never be thrown into company with him'.[3]

Believing they were the chosen people, chosen by God to be his favourites among all peoples, the Jews also segregated themselves from the Gentiles. They spoke disdainfully of them as 'the nations', an indiscriminate huddle of folk for whom they did not care enough to try to distinguish one from another. Certain extremists went so far as to say that it was illegal for a Jew to help a Gentile woman in childbirth, for that would mean bringing another Gentile into the world.

Their exclusive and disdainful attitude was one of the major causes of the anti-Jewish feeling so prevalent in the ancient world. It was also a contributary cause of many of the vindictive acts perpetrated against the Jews. On one occasion the Samaritans way-laid and killed some of the pilgrims journeying to Jerusalem for the Passover. Not content with this, they desecrated the Temple on the eve of the Passover by leaving the dead bodies in the sacred courts. To the Jews this was the most odious of all possible ceremonial pollutions. In AD 51 the hatred and spite between Jew and Samaritan became so intense that it flamed into civil war.

Substitute for 'Samaritan' the word 'Palestinian' and how modern it all is! It disturbed Jesus greatly that Jewish youngsters, instead of being nourished on the concept of the brotherhood of man, were being indoctrinated from an early age to hate rather than love the other nations of the world. Jesus also detested the labelling and pigeon-holing of social classes and religious groups.

It seared his very being that the feelings of orthodox Jews should have become so petrified that words like 'Samaritan' and 'Gentile' triggered off instinctive opposition and hatred. He felt impelled to side with those being maligned and unfairly treated, even though this meant that he himself was branded as outside the pale, and as a Samaritan, 'Samaritan' was in fact the worst name they could think of to call Jesus.

Jesus refused to accept that the problem of prejudice was too immense for anyone to do anything about. In his preaching he often praised the example of Samaritans and Gentiles. We might say he went out of his way to do so, but it would probably be truer to say that it was in accord with his way thus to speak and act. He instanced the ten lepers, only one of whom returned to say thanks, and he was a Samaritan.[4] In his famous parable of the Good Samaritan, the priest and the Levite passed by the wounded man. The Samaritan alone stopped to help.[5] When he preached in his home synagogue he pointed out how, long ago, when God needed lodgings for Elijah, he could not find them among the Jews, but had to go to the home of a Gentile.[6] He reminded them too, how, although there were many lepers in Israel, Elisha chose to heal Naaman, a Syrian.[7] It was to a Roman centurion that Jesus gave a grade 'A' for faith: 'I tell you, never in Israel have I found such faith'.[8] All this made his hearers very angry. The view that in God's sight other nations were as important as them was unacceptable. It still is for many.

Edwin Robertson tells of an Ashanti friend from Ghana. His attitude to the Gas was much the same as that of the Jews to the Samaritans. He found it impossible to think that any Ga could be good. When Edwin Robertson threatened to rewrite Jesus' parable and call it 'The Good Ga', his friend replied quite firmly, 'No Ga, man, woman or child, could ever be a Good Samaritan'.

Jesus' love and concern embraced the whole family of man. He included in the term 'neighbour' the very people whom many with their limited sympathies would like to exclude. 'Let God have blacks in his church if he wants them,' said a white South African. 'We sure don't want them in ours.' In God's kingdom depicted in Jesus' parables, tribe and race, rank and privilege count for nothing. In the parable of the great banquet[9] those who finally sit down at table are the disadvantaged and those discriminated against.

Basic also to the thinking of Jesus was the belief that no gift is superior or inferior to another. The person with the one talent is as important in the sight of God as the one with ten; the manual worker is as important as the white-collar worker. Jesus opposed all kinds of snobbery, including the snobbery of those who use their brains and tongues to highlight their superiority. Those who had difficulty expressing their thoughts were as important to Jesus as those who used polished sentences.

Words can be winked at, but not actions. That Jesus should speak well of Samaritans and foreigners and outcasts was bad enough. How much worse it was that he should practise what he preached by freely mixing with them. For a Jewish man to talk to a Jewish woman he did not know, was not done. For a Jewish man to talk to a Samaritan was frowned on. For a Jewish man to sit and talk to a Samaritan woman he did not know—that was an outrage. Yet that was what Jesus did by the well in Samaria.[10] When the Samaritan woman started back utterly surprised, Jesus sought to put her at her ease by doing what he did with Zaccheus. He asked for a favour that called for action. Glancing at her water-pot, he said, 'Would you give me a drink?' Jesus was prepared to go to great lengths and to endure slander, if only he could help break down the blind prejudice which he knew was, and still is, one of the main causes of deteriorating relationships in the various sectors of human society.

Occasionally when people speak prejudicially of Jews, Catholics or Black people, someone will come up with the classic line of defence: 'But look at Einstein, Pope John, Martin Luther King or Bishop Tutu', the implication being that Jews, Catholics and Blacks cannot therefore be all bad. Such defenders may mean well, but their approach is mistaken. Jesus knew that a minority group wants the right to have its ordinary folk, and not just its geniuses, acknowledged without prejudice.

Notes and References

1 John 8:48
2 Ezra 4:3
3 *Jesus the Messiah*, Edersheim, Vol 1, p 401
4 Luke 17:16
5 Luke 10:29f
6 Luke 4:26
7 Luke 4:27
8 Luke 7:9
9 Luke 14:15-24
10 John 4:8f

12

The Devil's Agent

What the Gospels call 'casting out devils' we might describe, rightly or wrongly, in other terms, but what cannot reasonably be doubted is that Jesus had power over those dark forces which ravage people's minds and cripple their bodies. The Jewish leaders would fain have denied his works of healing, but they could not. Walking the streets were blind people who could now see, lepers who had been cleansed, epileptics who had been cured and madmen now perfectly sane—all as a result of the healing ministry of Jesus. In almost every case, Jesus told those he cured that it was to God they should give the glory and thanks.

The Jewish leaders obviously had a problem of explanation on their hands. They were unwilling to concede that it was by the love and power of God that Jesus was able to conquer such mysterious mental and physical disorders. If he had been a man of God, he would have observed God's commandments. He would not have broken the Sabbath or those laws about fasting on special days. They finally concluded that the explanation of his unusual powers was that he was in league with Satan. 'It is by Beelzebub the prince of devils that he drives the devils out.'[1] An ugly rumour, yet a strange tribute! From the lips of his enemies as well as his friends, we get this picture of one who had power over disease, one who could 'drive out devils', one whose touch was life itself.

In the Gospels there is *not* the slightest indication that those who were conspiring to put Jesus to death were afraid that he might use his very real power to maim, that he might strike them blind or dumb. The absence of such fear on the part of his enemies, is surely a further unspoken tribute to the character of Jesus. Gethsemane proved them right. Jesus rebuked Peter when he lashed out with his sword at the soldiers. 'Put up your sword.'[2] Retaliation and revenge were anathema to Jesus. He would use his power only in the service of love. 'The Son of Man did not come to destroy men's lives, but to save them.'[3]

'A sorcerer in league with the devil.' Jesus sought to show the Pharisees how illogical their conclusion was. 'If Satan is divided against himself how can his kingdom stand?'[4] Would evil seek to cast out evil? But he reasoned in vain. They had prejudged the issue. This should surprise no one who realises that the strongest motives determining human behaviour are not those which spring from instincts such as sex and hunger, which we share with the animals, but those which spring from the desire to 'save face'.

'It is the practice of the multitude to bark at eminent men as little dogs do at strangers.'[5] Envy often eyes the more courageous or capable person with loathing. What low motives it often imputes. With what back-biting and sneers it expresses itself. Whoever heard jealous people passing scrupulously fair judgments on those who surpass them? It was because Mozart was fiercely jealous of Clementi, regarded by some as an even finer pianist, that he described Clementi's compositions as 'worthless' and his piano playing as having not a 'farthing's worth of feeling'.

The dark depths of the human heart, and the lengths to which envy will cause men to go, is nowhere better illustrated than in a letter which a Protestant minister, C. M. Hyde, who had worked in Honolulu, wrote to an Australian magazine about Father Damien:

> The simple truth is, he was a coarse, dirty man, head-strong and bigoted. He was not sent to Molokai, but went there without orders. . . . He was not a pure man in his relations with women, and the leprosy of which he died should be attributed to his vices. . . .

When this scurrilous letter was brought to the attention of
Robert Louis Stevenson, who knew and greatly admired Damien
and the work he had done for the lepers of Molokai, patiently
dressing their sores and stumps, being their gardener, cook and
grave-digger, he wrote a penetrating reply to Mr Hyde[6]:

> When leprosy descended and took root in the Eight Islands,
> what a glorious opportunity for your mission in Honolulu
> to do something about it, to show Christ-like concern. I
> know I am touching here upon a nerve acutely sensitive. I
> know that others of your colleagues look back on the inertia
> of your church, and the intrusive and decisive heroism of
> Damien with something almost to be called remorse. . . . I
> am persuaded your letter was inspired by a certain envy,
> not essentially ignoble. . . . You were thinking of the lost
> chance, the past day; of that which should have been
> conceived and was not; of the service due and not ren-
> dered. . . . But sir when we have failed and another has
> succeeded; when we have stood by and another has stepped
> in, when we sit and grow bulky in our charming mansions,
> and a plain uncouth peasant steps into the battle, under the
> eyes of God, and succours the afflicted and consoles the
> dying and is himself afflicted in his turn, and dies upon the
> field of honour, the battle cannot be retrieved as your
> unhappy irritation has suggested. It is a lost battle and lost
> forever. . . . You having failed and Damien succeeded, I
> marvel it should not have occurred to you that you were
> doomed to silence; that when you had . . . sat inglorious in
> the midst of your well-being, in your pleasant room, and
> Damien crowned with glories and horrors toiled and rotted
> in that pigsty of his under the cliffs of Kulawao—you, the
> elect who would not, were the last man on earth to collect
> and propogate gossip on the volunteer who would and did.

Character assassination is the readiest alternative for argument
that hard-pressed, jealous people have ever found. It is so easy to

deride, to find reasons to back up conclusions arrived at by prejudice. The more devoid people are of argument, the more inferior they feel, the more abominable the rumours they will spread. 'He is in league with the devil': such an attempt to smear the character of Jesus is further proof of his eminence. Had the Pharisees not felt inferior to Jesus, had they not been jealous of his power to heal, they would not have bothered to slander him. 'Mockery is the fume of little hearts.' [7]

Once, in the history of the French town of Chartres, the inhabitants wanted to destroy their magnificent cathedral. The reason given by one writer was that it revealed the poor design and shabbiness of all the other buildings in their foolish little city. Rather than improve what was unlovely, they contemplated destroying what was really lovely! It was similar with the Pharisees. Instead of being grateful for the healing ministry of Jesus, and seeking to reform their own lives and religion, their instinctive reaction was to destroy what was truly good and lovely. Thus the sharp contrast would no longer be noticeable. They even finally convinced themselves that there was nothing the world needed quite so much as to be rid of Jesus. It would be of great service to God! So they brought Jesus to Pilate and demanded his crucifixion.

Notes and References

1   Luke 11:15
2   Matthew 26:52
3   Luke 9:56
4   Luke 11:18
5   Seneca
6   An open letter to the Rev. Dr Hyde, February 25th 1890
7   'Idylls of the King'—Tennyson

13

The Befriender

'Friend of tax-gatherers and sinners'[1]: what sublime slander! How precious these words have become, words originally uttered to hurt and defile, the implication being that Jesus was like the company he kept. Throughout the Roman Empire, 'tax-gatherer' was a dirty word. The tax-gathering system lent itself to abuse. Though it might have been possible to do this necessary job honestly, it was the less scrupulous who applied. The extortion methods used, and the fact that in Palestine the tax was for a detested foreign government, resulted in Jewish tax-gatherers being ostracised. They were classed with highwaymen. Hence the derision Jesus aroused by freely associating with tax-gatherers and by including one among his chosen disciples.

To the dismay of respectable Jews, who thought in terms of rigid social and religious classes, Jesus also associated with rough, profane men like James and John, significantly nick-named 'sons of Thunder', and with women who eked out a hard living by easy virtue. When one such prostitute entered the home of Simon the Pharisee, and overcome with gratitude, washed Jesus' feet with her tears, Simon who was thoroughly respectable but unfeeling, recoiled lest she should happen to touch him. His mental comment was, 'If this fellow were a real prophet, he would know who this woman is that touches him'.[2] But Jesus did not hold himself aloof. Remember also the Samaritan woman[3] who came to Jacob's well at noon, an hour when no one else came. She had had five husbands and the man with whom she was living was not her husband. She came at that strange hour because she dreaded the hot words of her neighbours more than the hot rays of the sun. How pleasantly surprised she was when Jesus spoke to her.

I find it significant that the Gospel writers do not feel it necessary to defend the moral character of Jesus against Jewish attack. Most ministers today would not be able to survive three circumstantial and independent reports in the local paper that they had their feet or head kissed, scented and wiped by a woman of doubtful reputation. The lack of defensiveness with which the Gospel writers tell this story, and the story of his lengthy encounter with the Samaritan woman, surely tells us a great deal about the kind of person Jesus was.

'Friend of publicans and sinners': Jesus pleaded guilty to this charge of befriending those despised by 'respectable' society. Though guilt by association was as vicious a device then as it is now, Jesus was prepared to sit at table with the irreligious, and to be numbered with transgressors. On one occasion when the dubious character of his friends was pointed out to him, he said with a touch of irony, 'It is not the healthy who need a doctor, but the sick'.[4]

Though people's immoral and heartless behaviour grieved and hurt Jesus, it never put them beyond the reach of his love and concern. 'You see this woman?'[5] said Jesus to Simon the Pharisee. A simple question, yet what depths in it. Simon did not really see the woman. To him she was a type, a prostitute. That was her category and that was the end of it. Jesus on the other hand longed to harness for noble ends the strong passions, enthusiasms and ambitions of those who were socially outlawed. He also longed to provide the love, understanding and encouragement they craved, and needed.

Boris of Bulgaria used to alarm his royal court by insisting on mixing with common people. Into the streets he would go incognito, and mix with men and women, thereby in his unsettled country running a great risk. To his advisers who tried to stop him, he said, 'Before I can be their king, I must be their friend'. Such friendship was an integral part of Christ's ministry to the less attractive members of society, the lost sheep and the black sheep. As G. K. Chesterton once said, 'He never lost his taste for bad company'.

Jesus put human contact before religious contact. He did not say to the publicans and sinners, 'If you are prepared to listen to me and reform your ways, I will help you'; he began by befriending them. No one ever looked into those eyes without being certain that Jesus was really interested in him, that he was valued and taken seriously. 'Accept one another,' says Paul, '*as Christ accepted us.*'[6]

Behind labels like publican and sinner, Jesus saw people. He deemed everyone saint or sinner, rich or poor, learned or unlearned, worthy of his undivided attention. Whereas pseudo-important people make everybody else feel small, Jesus made those with whom he came into contact, feel important. He was genuinely concerned whether they sank or swam. Instead of poking about in the ashes of their personalities, he looked for the hidden nobilities, the flickering coals, in the hope of fanning them into a warm fire. The people of Jericho said of Zaccheus, 'He is a thief'.[7] Jesus said, 'He is a son of Abraham'.[8] Jesus saw the potential behind the greed. He knew that everyone has a deep need for positive human contact, for encouragement and love. Not surprisingly many left his presence changed people.

Though Jesus befriended tax-gatherers and sinners he never betrayed friendship by smiling at, or minimising, their shortcomings. He was well aware of the damage such sentimentality can cause. The trouble with the false testimonials people give themselves and others, is that they often finally come to believe them. King Lear suffered from an uncritical excess of self-love. His daughters Goneril and Regan, egotists like their father, were always ready with lying adulation. But Cordelia who really loved her father, would have no part in this sham. She knew he would never improve until he was willing to acknowledge the painful truth about himself. Jesus likewise kept stressing the need for people to be honest with themselves and God, to stop rationalising and excusing their conduct, thus making it seem better than they secretly knew it to be.

A common sentiment of our times sees delinquents as hapless victims of overwhelming circumstances or their genes, as being no more responsible for their actions than a thermometer is for frost. That is as mistaken as the dominant sentiment of the nineteenth century which arrogantly maintained that we are all 'Masters of our Fate', which refused to consider heredity or environment or extenuating circumstances. A teenager with a smattering of psychology concerned to absolve herself from moral blame, said, 'What can you expect? Look at the parents I had'. Since parents had parents too, and so back and on and on, are we to conclude that *no one* is ultimately responsible—not even heroin pushers, wife-beaters, slum landlords or excessively physical cops? Such a doctrine of inevitability is nowhere to be found in the teaching of Jesus. He never gave the impression that the feeling of guilt is a morbid delusion, or that wrongdoers were worrying themselves unnecessarily. He did not condone the unscrupulousness of tax-gatherers, or excuse the conduct of prostitutes. Concerning the woman in Simon's house who shed tears of penitence, who genuinely intended to break with her past, Jesus said, 'Her sins, *which are many*, are forgiven'.[9] His final words to the woman taken in adultery also have an astringence which rules out any suggestion of permissiveness. 'You may go; do not sin again.'[10]

Dr Lewis Thomas said of his psychiatric work, 'Therapy when it works is really plain friendship. The first recorded therapist, officially titled as such, was Patroclus, referred to by Homer as Achilles' "therapon". Patroclus was the leader's professional friend; he lived in the same tent, listened all day to Achilles' endless complaints, even encouraged him to shout out his anxieties, defended and represented his patient against the world, and finally perished in the performance of his duties. Therapy means standing by in steadfast, affectionate, and useful companionship'.[11] Little wonder that Jesus, the great befriender, was also a great therapist.

Notes and References

1 Luke 7:34
2 Luke 7:39
3 John 4:8f
4 Luke 5:32
5 Luke 7:44
6 Romans 15:7
7 Luke 19:8
8 Luke 19:10
9 Luke 7:47-48 (K. J.)
10 John 8:11
11 The Atlantic Monthly, April 1981.

14

The Carpenter

George Douglas, the author of that gripping novel of Scottish life, *The House with the Green Shutters,* reminds us how in a small village, 'every man knows everything to his neighbour's detriment. He can redd up his rival's pedigree, for example, and lower his pride (if need be) by detailing the disgraces of his kin. "I have grand news the day!" a big-hearted Scot will exclaim— "Jock Goudie has won the CB". "Jock Goudie," an envious bodie will pucker as if he had never heard the name—"Jock Goudie? Wha's he. . . . Oh ay, let me see now. He's a brother o' Drucken Will Goudie o' Auchter wheeze! Oo—ooh I ken him fine. His grannie keepit a sweetie-shop." ' [1]

Likewise some of the village people in Nazareth poured ridicule on Jesus' lowly station in life. He might have been a big-hit in the surrounding towns and villages, but not in Nazareth. The folks there could remember him when he was 'knee-high'. They were certain he was getting too big for his boots. 'Is not this the carpenter, the son of Mary, the brother of James and Joseph and Judas and Simon? Are not his sisters here with us?' [2] Thus they sought to dwarf his stature.

Such comments reinforce the impression we get from the Gospels that Jesus came from humble circumstances. I smiled recently when I heard of a mother and her ten year old son who were standing in front of Tintoretto's painting of 'The Nativity': 'Mummy, what I cannot understand is why God did not do better than have his own son born in a dirty old stable?' 'Well, you must remember,' said his mother, 'that Mary and Joseph were travelling a long way and the town was packed, and they were poor. . . .' 'They cannot have been poor,' the boy broke in, 'to get themselves painted by Tintoretto.' The mother was, however, right. Mary and Joseph were not well-off. The offering required of them for purification was 'a pair of turtle doves or two young pigeons',[3] the offering prescribed by Jewish law for those too poor to afford a lamb. But though Mary and Joseph were poor, pious exaggeration of their lowly circumstances serves no purpose save perhaps to arouse false emotions.

It is widely accepted that the reason that the Gospels say nothing of Joseph during Jesus' ministry is because his father died when Jesus was still an adolescent. As the eldest son, he would have had to work and provide for his mother and family until at least the younger members were able to fend for themselves. It was probably as a boy in Nazareth that Jesus learned that you cannot patch a well-worn coat, that had been handed down, with a new piece 'of unshrunk cloth',[4] a home truth which he was later to use to illustrate the relationship between the new Gospel and the old Judaism. There would also stick in his mind the day his mother turned the house upside down looking for a drachma she had lost—a coin worth a whole day's wages. She 'lit a lamp' and 'swept the house'[5] until she found it. These two phrases tell us quite a bit about the kind of working man's home in which Jesus was reared.

> The humbler Palestinian houses were very dark for they were lit by a little circular window only eighteen inches across. The broom was made of palm leaves. The search was difficult because there was no proper flooring, only the tramped down earth covered with dried reeds and rushes. It was not to clean the house that it was swept on this occasion. It was to dislodge the coin from its hiding place so that she would hear the tinkle of it, or catch the glint of it when it moved among the rushes.[6]

During his ministry, Jesus' financial position would certainly not improve. Joachim Jeremias points out[7] how rabbis and itinerant teachers were generally among the poorer classes. He quotes several examples from the second century. R. Gamaliel

II, who was renowned for his great learning, sometimes had not a bite to eat. Rabbi Akiba and his wife were so poor that they slept in straw during the winter; and the most often quoted Rabbi in the Mishnah, Rabbi Judah b. Eli, possessed only one cloak which he and his wife wore alternately when they went out. It was little different with Jesus. 'Foxes have their holes, the birds their roosts; but the Son of Man has nowhere to lay his head.'[8] At the end he owned nothing, and left nothing, but the clothes he wore. The controversy with the Pharisees concerning plucking heads of grain on the Sabbath,[9] is a further reminder that Jesus had little of this world's goods. The religious leaders were opposed to his doing this *on the Sabbath day,* not to the picking of the grains—for in Jewish law there was a humanitarian instruction that the hungry poor were allowed to pick grapes and heads of standing grain.[10]

In Jesus' parable of the Great Feast,[11] those invited first were people of standing and influence. They received advance invitations, for the higher you go in society, the more advance notice you need to be given. Important people have full diaries. Jesus did not belong to this elite. He did not, like one of his characters in another of his parables, dress in 'the finest linen'. Nor did he 'feast in great magnificence every day'.[12]

Although out of courtesy, Jesus was occasionally addressed as 'Rabbi' (a title for which he had no great liking, which he in fact asked his followers not to accept for themselves),[13] in the ordinary sense of the word, Jesus was not a rabbi. His education had been no more than what the local school, synagogue and his parents could provide. Yet despite this, ordinary folk hung on his words. He made a far greater impact on them than the qualified rabbis did. Unlike their own teachers, 'he taught with a note of authority'.[14] Jesus was more in the prophetic than the rabbinic tradition. 'In truth, in very truth I tell you. . . .'[15] Such personal authority startled synagogue congregations, accustomed to scribes who did little more than quote their teachers and their teachers' teachers.

People of wealth, fame, influence and education have little difficulty attracting an audience and getting publicity for their views on religious matters. The fact that Jesus, without any of the advantages of wealth, education or influential parents, should have made such an impressive impact, and that he, not Caiaphas, or Herod or Pilate, should have been the main talking point during the Passover,[16] would indicate that there must have been something extraordinary about his life and teaching.

The representatives of the established order made his humble circumstances and lack of education sufficient reason for dismissing what he taught. They made the elementary mistake of ascribing wisdom only to such as read many books and attend courses of lectures. People today make this same mistake when they equate having university degrees with having wisdom. The equation is not a valid one. Some graduates seem to become immaturer by degrees!

When in his parable about the rich farmer who built bigger and bigger barns, Jesus tells how God called the farmer 'a fool',[17] he did not mean that the man was stupid or retarded. The man had been no fool in the world of business. What Jesus meant was that he was totally lacking in discernment and true discrimination. There is that in life which ennobles and that which cheapens; there is that which puts you in harmony with yourself and others, with the world and God, and there is that which alienates you from the good in yourself, destroys your relationship with your fellows and with God. The farmer had lacked the ability to distinguish between them. He had been content with trivial and shallow answers to fundamental questions about life's destiny and meaning. His faith had been in the wrong things. He had foolishly imagined that the only things that matter are material things, and that the only things that count are those that can be counted.

The Jewish leaders judged Jesus by the wrong tests. They had forgotten what their prophets and wise men had taught, that reverence is the principal part of wisdom and that there is no direct correlation between wisdom and fame or wealth. Just as in music and art, sensitivity is the beginning of musical ability and artistic competence, so sensitivity towards God is the beginning of a true understanding of life. Wisdom comes from being in rapport with the mind and spirit of God, from having a sincere desire to do what God would have us do, even when it does not suit our plans or fulfil our ambitions. It is found in those whose hearts are pure, who see life through the eyes of caring love, who have the greatest capacity for moral judgment and the greatest insight into the deep things of God.

Though Jesus came from a lowly background, and had never enjoyed the benefits of 'further education', he fulfilled all the conditions for true wisdom. Even when scorn and ridicule were heaped upon him, he did not waver from the way of caring love. His burning desire was to do what God wanted: 'It is meat and drink for me to do the will of him who sent me'.[18] Was there ever such rapport with the mind and spirit of God? Was there ever such astute discernment of what motivates people, or such profound reverence for God's world? Three books were ever open before Jesus—the Old Testament, Nature and Man. Every page of the New Testament attests that he had read well in all three.

Notes and References

1   p 47
2   Mark 6:3
3   Luke 2:24
4   Mark 2:21
5   Luke 15:8
6   *And Jesus said,* W. Barclay, p 173
7   *Jerusalem in the Time of Jesus*
8   Matthew 8:20
9   Matthew 12:1
10 Deuteronomy 23:24,25
11 Luke 14:15f
12 Luke 16:19

13 Matthew 23:8
14 Mark 1:22
15 John 1:51
16 John 7:10f
17 Luke 12:16f
18 John 4:34

15

The Saviour

Bernard Shaw's character St Joan says, 'O God who made this beautiful earth, when will it be ready to receive thy saints?' Five hundred years before the birth of Christ, Isaiah concerned himself with this same question. In a world where selfishness, injustice, pride and hatred are firmly established, Isaiah knew that reformers who challenged the *status quo* would almost certainly suffer. If in the interests of greater honesty, justice and brotherliness anyone dared to interfere with other people's privileges, or exposed their prejudices, or proved to be a threat to their profits, he would be 'cut off out of the land of the living'.[1] His grave would be with the wicked. The life of Jesus verified Isaiah's profound insight. He was despised and rejected. He was put to death with criminals. Not content with this, his enemies jeered and mocked as he hung on the Cross. 'He saved others, but he cannot save himself.'[2] These words were intended as a cruel taunt, and yet what a tribute! Even those who hated Jesus had to admit that he had healed and helped many. Even from the mouths of those who crucified him, we get a picture of one who went about doing good. 'He saved others.'

It was with a sigh of relief that the Jewish hierarchy saw Jesus nailed to the Cross. Son of God indeed! They had finally put an end to such blasphemous speech. Where was his power now? The fool had been deluded. 'Himself he cannot save.' Had they understood the principle that only by losing self can you help others, only by giving life can you bless, they might have said reverently, 'He saved others, therefore he could not save himself'.

A mediaeval painter depicts Jesus on the Cross with one arm disengaged, reaching down to lift a spectator who had stumbled. Such artistic licence is justified, for even on the Cross, despite his own suffering, Jesus' prime concern was the welfare of others. His first prayer was for those who crucified him, 'Father forgive them'.[3] Later, to the thief he said, 'To-day you shall be with me in paradise'.[4] To John he entrusted the care of his mother.[5] The breadth and depth of Jesus' concern for others was in fact one of his most striking characteristics. It disturbed him greatly that no provision should be made for those in Palestine who could not fight their own battles—that the blind and the crippled should be left to beg by the wayside—that widows and orphans should have to sell themselves into slavery. Caring love was the dominant theme of his parables, the explanation of his miracles. He healed people, not to impress, nor to prove his Messiah-ship, but because he was 'moved with compassion'.[6] The Greek word which is used—*splagchnizesthai*—comes from the Greek word for bowels. Jesus was moved in the depth of his being. Jesus' life reveals the costliness of caring love. Had he not insisted on dining with the wrong people, he could have saved his reputation. Had he not protested against simple folk being fleeced and short-changed in the temple, had he not sought to reform Judaism, he could have saved himself the agony of crucifixion. Lord Braxfield, the nineteenth century Scottish Judge, was extremely conservative. He detested all radicals and reformers. When a Mr Gerard sought to remind Lord Braxfield that Jesus had been a reformer, back came the reply, 'Muckle he made o' that. He was hangit'.[7] Though said in derision, what a strange compliment! If we define a radical, as Webster's dictionary does, as 'one who favours fundamental change', then Jesus was a radical. Concerned to save others from what degraded and spoilt life, he could not save himself. He was hangit.

Dr Paul Tournier tells how he and his wife noticed that nearly always when they quarrelled at night, it was at the end of a day in which they had been drained emotionally trying to comfort anxious people or reconcile estranged couples.[8] When the ill woman in the crowd touched the hem of Jesus' garment, Jesus knew that strength had been drained from him.[9] On another occasion, Jesus was so physically, mentally and spiritually exhausted, through having identified himself with others and their problems, that not even a wild storm on the lake awakened him.[10]

To invest one's life as Jesus did in other lives, to stand by the sorely tempted, to acknowledge one's essential brotherhood even with those temperamentally and socially incompatible, to 'love the unloved', to protest against what dehumanises people, can upset self-centred plans. Young ministers, doctors, nurses, and social workers are sometimes told they must learn to confront grievous situations unemotionally. To learn this art might save emotional wear and tear, but there would be little healing or comfort. If they are to be effective, they cannot avoid being affected.

Aware that they would have to take pains to lessen pain, many live in that state which psychologists call 'affectlessness'. They read hunger and loneliness statistics, but without compassion. Many likewise refuse to forgive. 'People might take advantage,' they say. Perhaps they would. Jesus knew his goodwill might be spurned. He knew that he would not quickly correct other people's spite and meanness with forgiveness and caring love. But he also knew he would not correct it in any other way.

According to Jesus, the acid test of our concern is not glib pronouncement, but costly participation. It involves doing some positive good for people from whom we are estranged in an attempt to diminish the hate and bitterness in the world. It involves bridling our own will that a will greater than our own might be done, and so that needs greater than our own might be met. Jesus conceived prayer not as an opportunity to get God into our hands, but rather the means whereby we put our lives unreservedly into God's hands.

> Hallowed be Thy name, *not mine,*
> Thy kingdom come, *not mine,*
> Thy will be done, *not mine.*[11]

Whereas the supreme concern of many is to push themselves forward, to get their own way, sit on their own moneybags and extend their little empire, the supreme concern of Jesus was that God's name should be honoured, His kingdom advanced and His will done. Those who hoard life, who refuse to share or care or get involved in any cause bigger than themselves, do save themselves many a criticism, hurt and sleepless night, but in the process they die emotionally and spiritually. When life has no meaning beyond its own narrow horizons, it grows emptier and emptier. The most tragic funerals are without doubt those of people who never really lived, because they never really loved. At the heart of every paradise that people seek to build for themselves, is a serpent trying to turn it into a fool's paradise. The name of that serpent is I, alias 'my' and 'mine', a self preoccupied with its own claims and needs.

On the other hand, although life becomes more demanding when we are concerned to save others, when we assume responsibility for elderly neighbours and community activities, it also becomes richer and more friendly. God, as Jesus reminded us, has created life in such a way that whoever would save his life will lose it and whoever loses his life will save it. [12] We all need to feel of use. There is ultimately no greater satisfaction than that of standing with God against the darkness in people's lives, doing the little we can to help and then slowly watching the dawn come.

In scene after scene in the Gospels, the dominant impression is that of life released, freed from the self-centredness which hems it in and detracts from it. Jesus did save many others. Wherever he went, horizons were broadened and lives enlarged. He set people free to be the selves God meant them to be.

Notes and References

1   Isaiah 53

2 Mark 15:31
3 Luke 23:34
4 Luke 23:43
5 John 19:27
6 Mark 1:41
7 Observer Supplement, November 1974
8 *Doctor's Casebook*
9 Luke 8:46
10 Luke 8:23
11 Salvation Army Cadet Oath
12 Matthew 10:39

16

The King

What a laugh, the soldiers thought—this fellow with his hands tied, charged with being a king. Still it was a jest worth carrying on. 'Let us try and make him look a bit more like a king.' So they seized an old faded scarlet tunic and put it on his lacerated shoulders. This would serve for the royal purple. For a sceptre they handed him a reed that was lying nearby. 'What about a crown?' One of them remembered there was a thorn bush outside. So he cut off some branches, wove them into a crown, and came and crushed them on the brow of Jesus. 'That's better now. The fellow looks a bit more like a king.' So down on their knees they got and cried, 'Hail king of the Jews'.[1] Then rising, they slapped him on the face; deep down these soldiers despised the Jews.

'King of the Jews'—it was a joke with the soldiers, but one wonders whether with Pilate there was not a deeper reason for placing these words at the top of the Cross. Though this super-scription—the first words ever written about Jesus—may have been nailed to the Cross to mock the Jewish leaders, to turn the whole Jewish nation into a wayside sneer—it was certainly not put there to mock Jesus. Pilate seems to have been impressed by this Galilean. Perhaps he wished the Jews had a king like this. He could not honestly believe that in front of him stood a serious competitor either to himself as Procurator, or to Tiberius as Emperor. If Jesus really had been a militant champion of inde-pendence, a fanatical nationalist, the Jews would have been supporting him—not demanding his crucifixion!

Orthodox Jews believed that God was *the* King above all Kings. In many ways the idea of kingship in Israel was quite different from that in other nations. The Jews never regarded their king as an absolute ruler who could do as he pleased. In fact the Jews so stressed the sovereignty of God that for a long time they had no earthly king. But finally in the days of the prophet Samuel, around the year 1030BC, the Jews realised their need for someone to lead them against the Philistines. They realised too their need of central authority to give order and coherence to the twelve tribes. And so the elders of Israel came to Samuel saying, 'Appoint us a king to govern us like other nations'.[2] But God was still to be regarded as *the* King. 'The Lord is king forever and ever,'[3] says the Psalmist. 'The holy one of Israel is our king.'[4] These come near to being one-sentence statements of the faith of Israel. It was because Jezebel realised that it was this belief in the absolute sovereignty of God which severely limited the powers of her husband King Ahab, that she sought to destroy the Jewish faith. Back in Tyre from where she had come, the king was a King. There his subjects did as he ordered. There Naboth would not have dared say 'No' to the monarch.

In the time of Jesus, Jews longed for the day when God would show himself king over all the earth, when He would send his specially-anointed representative, the Messiah, who would be one even greater than King David, who would free the Jews from the overlordship of Rome. Jesus taught that this divine intervention was no longer a shining hope of the far horizon, but a reality now. Mark tells us how 'Jesus came into Galilee proclaiming the Gospel of God: "The time has come; the Kingdom of God is upon you".'[5] Jesus accepted the concept of Messianic kingship—and immediately transformed it.

During an adult Bible Class, a teacher asked how the group felt they might recognise Jesus were he to return. One woman said, 'I'd know him by the glory round his head'. But Jesus had no glory round his head. He came incognito. We misunderstand the kingship of Jesus if we think of it as Jezebel did. The Swedish model of kingship is more helpful. In Sweden the king is a commoner who has a royal office—he embodies royalty, he exercises it. You may see him in the street any day. There is nothing to see but another man, yet you have seen the king. Likewise in Jesus, men and women were confronted with a king who spoke of the hungry and thirsty, strangers and prisoners as his brothers and sisters. No king was ever less concerned about looking like a king. Though Jesus was well aware that many are greatly influenced by what is outwardly impressive and spectacular, that the pageant of authority often commands the homage of the gallery, yet that was not his way. In the Upper Room shortly before his death, he gave his disciples an unforgettable picture of his kind of kingship. Taking a towel and a basin, he became a servant, and did for the disciples what they refused to do for each other. He washed their feet. He was a king with a towel on his arm, and a basin for a sceptre.

Pascal once compared the great conquerors of this world and the great reformers—people like Alexander the Great—with people like Archimedes. He pointed out how Archimedes fought no battles. He did nothing to draw attention to himself—and yet his passion for truth, and his discoveries, live and serve the world still. 'Though he did not catch the eye, how he blazed out before the mind.' That was also Christ's way, not the way of outward show or compulsion, but of lowly service, and quiet persuasion.

The Kingdom of God was central to the message of Jesus. It is in the context of the Kingdom that all his words and actions must be interpreted. The miracles are signs of the Kingdom; the parables and other teachings describe life in the kingdom and the conditions of membership.

Dr Moffatt's phrase, 'the Reign of God', conveys the meaning more accurately, for today phrases like the 'ancient kingdom of Dalriada', or even 'my kingdom for a horse', have a territorial connotation. The basic idea of the Kingdom, as Jesus used it, was not geographical or political. The throne of God, he implied, was the human heart. Whenever anyone acknowledges that Jesus is Lord and wherever God's will is done, there we have the Kingdom.

An important passage for understanding the idea of the Reign of God is the one where, in reply to Jesus' question 'Who do you say that I am?', Peter said 'You are the Messiah, the son of the living God'.[6] Here Peter seeks to make articulate what, during their time together, he had come to feel about Jesus. With this first public recognition of the Lordship of Christ, the Kingdom could be said to have come. 'You are Peter, the Rock; and on this rock I will build my Church.'[7] In other words, upon people with your insight and faith, people willing to give me the loyalty they would give an earthly king, I will build my Church. The kind of loyalty involved is nowhere better illustrated than in the words of an obscure Old Testament figure by the name of Ittai. On a dark day, when many of David's troops were choosing to desert their chief, David turned to Ittai and said in effect, 'Look you have got it made at home. Why don't you go back? You've served us well'. But Ittai answered, 'As the Lord lives ... wherever you may be, in life or in death, I your servant will be there'.[8]

We understand the parables of the Kingdom—the parable about buying the pearl of great price,[9] and the parable about finding treasure in a field and selling all to purchase it[10]—only when we realise that Jesus is the pearl and the treasure. He, and the things he stood for, are the most important realities in the world. It is significant that after Jesus' death, the Gospel of the Kingdom became the Gospel of Christ. In the minds of the early disciples the two were the same.

An American who was tried for being a conscientious objector to the Vietnam war, carefully explained his reasons. The judge listened to the end, but then said, 'Your position would be logical if the Kingdom of God had come. But it hasn't'. Quickly and quietly the lad replied, 'It has for me'. Though primarily a relationship between God and the individual, the Kingdom ultimately appears in the world as a society of people linked together by the fact of their common allegiance to the one King. The gospel of the Kingdom has social implications.

In the parable of the mustard seed,[11] the final luxuriant foliage of the mustard plant in which the birds build their nests, suggests an extension of the kingdom out of all proportion to its humble beginnings. In the parable of the yeast,[12] the reign of God in men's hearts is likened to a ferment which gradually penetrates and affects the whole, changing and ennobling the assumptions upon which people live their lives.

When the son of the famous German theologian, Adolph Von Harnack, was waiting for execution at the hands of the Nazis, one of his fellow-prisoners, an accomplished violinist, was given permission to play for him. Young Harnack requested the triumphant hymn, 'The standards of the King go forward', written in the sixth century when an earlier barbarism had overtaken Europe and engulfed the Church in paganism. Harnack believed that as the standards of the King had gone forward then, they would also prevail against the darkness of Nazism. He believed that evil, although often aggressive, and apparently victorious, cannot finally defeat God's purposes. His remarkable inner poise stemmed from his conviction that love is ultimately stronger than hate, goodness more powerful than evil, that truth will outlast lies, and that death has lost its sting. Evil men may set fire to the universe, but at its core the universe is fireproof. The New Testament speaks of the 'dethroned powers who rule this world'.[13] The decisive issue was settled at Calvary. There is only one throne, and it is occupied by the Risen Christ.

In *Starling of the White House,* we read of how Woodrow Wilson, the champion of the League of Nations, following his campaign in 1916 for a second term as President, was on the presidential yacht, the *Mayflower,* awaiting the returns from the various states. While these were being received, Mr Wilson finally went to sleep. Later that night Mr Starling, who had been on the White House staff for many years, learned that Mr Wilson had been re-elected. His comments are significant: 'The boss had been re-elected and was in for a rough time. However unimportant, I was a member of the team. Suddenly I realised that I was a Wilson man—that I believed in the things for which he stood—that I would follow him wherever he led. Standing in the galley of the *Mayflower* in the darkness before the dawn of that November morning, I realised that the man on the boat stood for something bigger than myself, bigger than himself, bigger than America. He stood for the hope of the world'.

Whether or not Woodrow Wilson merited such glowing epithets, it is certainly in that spirit that Christians ought to relate themselves to Jesus Christ, to someone bigger than themselves; someone bigger than any branch of the Church; bigger than the world itself—King of kings and Lord of lords, the champion of the family of nations, the hope of the world. The all-important issue is not whether we will succeed in establishing his Kingdom on earth, but whether we are prepared to live as his grateful and obedient servants, whether we are prepared to put our lives under his marching orders.

When the Jews later came to Pilate and said, concerning the notice which was hung on the Cross, 'You should not write, "King of the Jews", write rather, "He claimed to be the king of the Jews"', Pilate replied, 'What I have written I have written'.[14]

The centuries have shown that, whatever Pilate's reason was for writing this superscription, never were truer words written.

Notes and References

1 John 19:3
2 1 Samuel 8:5
3 Psalm 10:16
4 Psalm 89:18
5 Mark 1:14,15
6 Matthew 16:16
7 Matthew 16:18
8 2 Samuel 15:21
9 Matthew 13:46
10 Matthew 13:44

11 Matthew 13:31
12 Matthew 13:33
13 1 Corinthians 2:6 (Moffatt)
14 John 19:22